Exploring Our Lives

A Writing Handbook for Senior Adults

by Francis E. Kazemek

 S A N T A
M O N I C A
P R E S S

Published by:
Santa Monica Press LLC
P.O. Box 1076
Santa Monica, CA 90406-1076
1-800-784-9553
www.santamonicapress.com
books@santamonicapress.com

Printed in the United States

Santa Monica Press books are available at special quantity discounts when purchased in bulk by corporations, organizations, or groups. Please call our Special Sales department at 1-800-784-9553.

ISBN 1-891661-26-4

Library of Congress Cataloging-in-Publication Data

Kazemek, Francis E.
        Exploring our lives : a writing handbook for senior adults / by Francis E. Kazemek.
                p. cm.
        ISBN 1-891661-26-4
        1. English language—Rhetoric—Handbooks, manuals, etc. 2. Autobiography—Authorship—Handbooks, manuals, etc. 3. Autobiographical memory—Handbooks, manuals, etc. 4. Reminiscing in old age—Handbooks, manuals, etc. 5. Creative writing—Handbooks, manuals, etc. 6. Authorship—Handbooks, manuals, etc. I. Title.

PE1408 .K36 2002
808'.042—dc21

                                                                        2002009148

"You Reading This, Be Ready" copyright 1998 by the Estate of William Stafford. Reprinted from *The Way It Is: New & Selected Poems* with the permission of Graywolf Press, Saint Paul, Minnesota.

Book and cover design by Lynda "Cool Dog" Jakovich

Contents

Honoring Memory

. . . memory is a kind
of accomplishment,
a sort of renewal . . .

The American doctor-poet William Carlos Williams wrote the above lines late in his life as he reflected upon the role and importance of memory. Memory, he insisted in many of the poems he wrote in his 70s, is more than nostalgia for the "good old days." Certainly it involves a looking backwards, a life review, but it also is a looking forward, a new viewing of what we may have taken for granted for many years. Memory is a creative act, and as such we all have the potential to be creative artists.

Here is part of a story by a woman who was 92 years old when she wrote it. In her story she recounts her family's move from a comfortable city home to an undeveloped rural area during the First World War.

> *My mother was very lonesome. There were no nearby neighbors to visit. There were only us kids from day to day. All the water had to be brought in from the well. We bathed in a wash tub, used an outdoor "biffy," and also used kerosene lamps which had to be filled and cleaned each day.*
>
> *My mother's life was changed completely, and her daily life became more difficult because of these hardships.*
>
> *She had little say in the move. She simply listened to my father. Things were different in those days.*

The writer is remembering a key event in her family's life, but she is doing more than that. She is seeing through eight decades and re-creating her mother's loneliness, hardships, and sadness over leaving her neighborhood and friends back in the city. After all these years, her mother's feelings still exist and are acknowledged as important not only to the writer but to anyone who reads the story. This creative act of seeing the past with understanding and imagination honors the memory of the writer's mother.

This book is about honoring memory, yours and those of others. Its purpose is to help you capture and shape memories into a variety of written forms: stories, poems, memoirs, and more. It is also about exploring your daily personal life through diaries and the recording of dreams.

You most likely have your own particular purpose for reading this book. Perhaps you want to put into print those oral history tapes that you or others have recorded and to which no one listens. Maybe you would like to try your hand at writing poetry and are looking for some practical suggestions on how to get started. Perhaps you want to capture significant events of your life as a legacy for your family and friends. Or perhaps, as one woman said in one of my writing workshops, you simply want to write memorable stories for your grandchildren.

Whatever your reasons for reading this book, you will find it immediately helpful and practically useful. It will guide you with many examples and specific instructions as you put your memories and ideas on paper. But more, it will encourage you to try your hand at different kinds of writing that perhaps you have never attempted before.

In over twenty years of conducting writing workshops with Seniors, I have found again and again that people who are convinced they can write only biographical stories in prose are surprised and excited at their latent ability to write poetry, fictional short stories, and children's books.

Looking at a particular events in our lives, say, our first love, through a written memoir, short story, or poem gives us various angles from which to see the event. Each kind of writing offers a different insight and the kind of renewal that William Carlos Williams describes in his poem. I hope as you read this book you will try forms of writing that might be new or even strange to you. I guarantee that you'll be delighted with the results.

This book is arranged in various chapters, each of which presents a different kind of writing. I suggest that you take a little time to look through the Contents and perhaps read the Introduction to each chapter. This will give you an overall understanding of the book's scope and might even intrigue you to consider forms of writing which you typically don't use.

Once you have a sense of the book's arrangement, I recommend that you read and work through the chapters in the order I have arranged them. Of course you may choose to skip around, and that's fine. However, I have made various connections between and among the chapters, and working through them, or at least reading through them, in order will help you better see these connections. Let's begin.

CHAPTER ONE

Getting Started

Introduction

My purpose in this chapter is twofold: to get you writing immediately, and to introduce you to the format I use in the rest of the book. You quickly will see that it's not only easy to start writing, but that you can write about anything—even the most seemingly insignificant thing.

Writing about Objects

Here's a short poem by the American poet, Carl Sandburg. It's titled "Street Window":

The pawn-shop man knows hunger,
And how far hunger has eaten the heart
Of one who comes with an old keepsake.
Here are wedding rings and baby bracelets,
Scarf pins and shoe buckles, jeweled garters,

Old-fashioned knives with inlaid handles,
Watches of old gold and silver,
Old coins worn with finger-marks.
They tell stories.

All of those objects that are special to us and perhaps to no one else, all of those rings, pins, knives, keepsakes, and whatnot, they all tell particular stories. To begin, let's try writing about a couple of particular objects: one of yours and one of mine. I'd like you to follow along writing about your object as I write about mine.

Select an Object

Choose an object that is important to you in some way or that holds special memories for you. Look around your house, in your dresser drawers, or perhaps even on your own person. Maybe the thing you select is a cameo bracelet or pin, a dish handed down to you by your grandmother, a piece of pottery you purchased on a special vacation, a brightly-colored stone you found at the seashore, a piece of furniture, or a cross-stitch hanging created by one of your children. *It is important that you have the object in front of you so that you can explore it!*

I've selected the watch that I wear daily. Now get a blank sheet of paper and list your object.

My Object
My father's watch

Looking Closely at the Object

Examine your object closely. Look at it from different angles. Turn it around in different ways if you can or walk around it. Look at the smallest parts and those aspects that make it unique. Feel it. Smell it. Listen to it if you can. Taste it if that's possible. *Nothing is insignificant!* On your sheet of paper make a list of words or phrases that simply describe what your see, feel, smell, hear, and taste.

My Object

My father's watch
Gruen Veri-Thin Precision
Silver case
Black minute and hour hands
Red second hand
Military time: 1 to 12 in silver outer ring, 13 to 24 in black inner ring
60 second marks in black in most outer ring
Rust spots on face
Cracked crystal
Wind-up watch
"Helen to Frank 46026339" engraved on back
Ticking is loud
Edges of case nicked, scarred, and rough when I rub them
Tastes metallic like a fork
Smells like metal that's been wet and rusted in the past

List as many words or phrases as you can that describe your object. Try to list at least ten to twenty.

What we've just done is simply to describe *What* our objects are. This is one of the "Reporter's 5 Ws & H" questions: *Who, What, Where, When, Why,* and *How.* Let's do the others. Once again, use my list as an example.

Other Things About the Object

My Object
My father's watch
Gruen Veri-Thin Precision
Silver Case
Black minute and hour hands
Etc.

Who
My father
Construction worker
Died in 1977 at age 61
Born and lived in Chicago
A young hobo during the Great Depression
Work-callused hands
Strong, knobby wrists

When
My mother gave it to him when he left for WWII: "Helen to Frank"

Where
My mother gave it to him in Chicago
My father wore it for over 30 years
I've worn it around the USA & the world since

How

I got it when my father died
It was on his chest of drawers

Why

It's important to me because it reminds me of my father
It's a connection between my father and mother
It's a connection between them and me
It's a symbol of my father's strength
It represents a way of life rapidly fading

Some of the words and phrases that you list under *Who, What, Where, When, Why,* and *How,* of course, can also be listed under more than one of these categories. For example, I put "I got it when my father died" under *How,* but I also could have put it under *When.* Where you place particular words and phrases is not as important as the fact that the more you describe, reflect upon, and list about your object the better.

Try a First Draft

Let's try a simple paragraph about our objects using the lists of *Who, What, Where, When, Why,* and *How* that we've created. We won't use everything on our lists; indeed, we may only use a small number of our words and phrases, but it's better to have too much to work with than not enough. And as we begin to write we also might discover that new words and ideas come to mind.

I want the first sentence of my paragraph to grab the reader's attention. Thus, I want to make it as particular and interesting as possible. Notice how the following first sentences become more specific:

I found my father's watch when he died. I found my father's Gruen wristwatch when he died. I found my father's Gruen Veri-Thin wristwatch on the chest of drawers after his funeral.

Now on your paper try to write at least three opening sentences. Select one that you like.

Have you selected a sentence? Fine. Don't worry about it being too short or "not good enough." Right now we just want to get started with our writing.

I want to further describe the watch so I'll look at my lists and add some additional information.

I found my father's Gruen Veri-Thin wristwatch on the chest of drawers after his funeral. My mother had given it to him when he left for Army boot camp in 1945. She had the jeweler engrave "Helen to Frank" and his service number "46026339" on the back.

Using your lists, add a couple more sentences describing your object. Once again, use particular describing words. Take your time. We're in no hurry. Once you have two or three more sentences, we'll continue.

Since I love this watch because it is a symbol of my father, I'm going to open my second paragraph by comparing it to him.

The case is as nicked, scarred, and rough as my father's life had been. Hobo, construction worker, boozer, brawler, husband, and father of six, he often kept the wrong time with his family and friends—his spirit as cracked as the crystal on his knobby wrist.

I've made a decision here in my writing to use the object, the wristwatch, as a catalyst to describe my father. I could have moved in another direction, but this seems "right" to me now. Notice how, as I was writing, new words and phrases came to my mind that were not on my original lists, for example, "boozer" and "brawler." Notice how I used words on my list, "cracked crystal," to make a comparison to my father: "his spirit as cracked as the crystal on his wrist."

Using your lists and perhaps adding additional words or phrases, write at least two more sentences about your object.

Now that you have a couple of paragraphs about your object, read them *out loud.* It's important for us to *hear* how our writing sounds. Quite often by hearing what we've written, we're able to see what changes we might—or need to—make in order to create the most lively and vivid piece.

We can write a great more about our objects, but my purpose here is to simply get you writing and for you to see it's easy to begin. So let's end the short sketches of our objects with a closing paragraph.

My object sketch is about my father and how by wearing his watch I carry something of him, of his spirit, with me. I want my final paragraph to express this connection, and I want it to be as vivid and interesting to the reader as my opening sentences. Going back to my lists and considering what I've written up to this point, I'm going to try the following:

The rust stains on its face grow darker and more alive
when it rains. At such times I often hold the wristwatch to
my ear and listen to its heartbeat. I smile and whisper to
myself, "Dad."

Since I want to convey the fact that the wristwatch represents an everyday connection between me and the spirit of my
father, notice how I have given the watch human characteristics:
it becomes "more alive"; I listen to its "heartbeat"; and I
whisper "Dad" when I listen to it. I made all of these decisions
based on my primary *purpose* for writing this short object
sketch, and that is, to express the symbolic importance of my
father's wristwatch to me. As I wrote, I used the lists I had generated, but other words, phrases, and ideas came to my mind.
They will also come to you as you write. The very act of writing
awakens our subconscious and even our unconscious minds.

Look at what you have written up to this point, look again
at the lists you have created, and consider the primary point
of your short object sketch. Then try a final paragraph of a
few sentences which will bring your sketch to a conclusion.
Once again, try to be vivid in your closing.

Looking Again at Our First Drafts

What you should now have is a first draft of your particular
object sketch. Here's what mine looks like:

I found my father's Gruen Veri-Thin wristwatch on the
chest of drawers after his funeral. My mother had given it to
him when he left for Army boot camp in 1945. She had the

jeweler engrave "Helen to Frank" and his service number "46026339" on the back.

The case is as nicked, scarred, and rough as my father's life had been. Hobo, construction worker, boozer, brawler, husband, and father of six, he often kept the wrong time with his family and friends—his spirit as cracked as the crystal on his knobby wrist.

The rust stains on its face grow darker and more alive when it rains. At such times I often hold the wristwatch to my ear and listen to its heartbeat. I smile and whisper to myself, "Dad."

Many writers maintain that the hardest part of writing is working with the first draft, or revising what we have written. That's often true, but it depends on what we want to do with the piece of writing with which we're working. You'll always want to look again at your first draft to see if there is anything that will make it more descriptive, interesting, and coherent— revision, or "re-vision," literally means "to see again." However, sometimes, depending on your purpose, you might tinker a little bit with your first draft but then leave it as you first wrote it.

My purpose in this chapter is not to focus on revision; we'll deal with that in more detail in a later chapter. However, let's try just for some practice at least one or two small changes to our object sketches.

I've re-read my object sketch several times, and for the most part I like it. However, something about the sentence "The rust stains on its face grow darker and more alive when it rains" doesn't seem right to me. The stains do seem more alive when it's raining or when there's high humidity, but they really do not grow darker. I realize that what I was trying to do was to add more descriptive words simply for their own sake. The words "grow darker" are not necessary; thus,

I'm going to delete them from my sketch. The sentence now reads: "The rust stains on its face come alive when it rains."

I've also looked at my first sentence again: "I found my father's Gruen Veri-Thin wristwatch on the chest of drawers after his funeral." I actually found the wristwatch on *his* chest of drawers; thus, I think it's better if I change "the" to "his." This makes my first sentence more particular and more personal. It now reads: "I found my father's Gruen Veri-Thin wristwatch on his chest of drawers after his funeral."

Re-read your sketch a couple of times. See where you might be able to take out at least *one* word or phrase that is not necessary. Or you might see where adding a word or phrase would help improve your sketch. Make at least *one* change, and then we'll leave our object sketches.

Review of What We've Done

Let's review what we've done so far.

First, we've selected some object that we really wanted to write about, something that has importance to us. Why write about things we don't care too much about? Life is too short to waste it in such a manner

Second, before we started writing we spent some time examining, thinking about, and listing words and phrases about our objects. Sometimes we might have an idea in our mind and simply want to start writing, but, in general, it's better to spend at least a little time brainstorming ideas, words, and phrases on paper before we actually begin writing. We used the Reporter's 5Ws & H (*Who, What, Where, When, Why,* and *How)* as a guide to help us explore our objects.

Third, we used words and phrases from our lists to construct an opening sentence. We tried to make our first sentence descriptive, particular, and vivid enough to capture the reader's attention.

Fourth, as we wrote our object sketches we not only used our lists of words and phrases but we also added new words and phrases that came to mind. We saw that the act of writing helped us to generate new ideas.

Fifth, we read out loud what we had written. Saying our writing out loud helps us get a sense of the piece's rhythm and often highlights possible changes.

Sixth, once we had a first draft we went back and looked at it again to see if there were ways in which we might make it clearer, stronger, and more interesting. We saw that by "re-visioning" our piece, by seeing it again, we might be able to improve it.

Seventh, we might now put away our object sketches and let them "incubate" for a while, or we might give them to someone to read. Depending upon our purpose for writing a piece and our intended audience, we might share our writing with others immediately or we might simply put it away for further reflection and writing.

This is the format that I will use loosely throughout the book. You will see variations on it, for example, different ways of generating ideas, but we will try to follow this structure whether we're writing object sketches, memoirs, or poetry. In addition, I will use the Reporter's 5Ws & H as a way of structuring subsequent chapters.

Let's Try One More

Before we move on to the next chapter, let's try one more object sketch using the same step-by-step process we followed above. I'll let you do this on your own. Relax and take your time. Remember to write about an object that you care about or something that triggers important memories. Here are a couple of object sketches written at various times by two women in my workshops. One is short and the other more detailed. They will provide you with additional examples of object sketches and perhaps trigger ideas of your own.

The Green Rocker Chair

The green rocker chair is an old rocking chair. The arms look like the beak of a bird. They are red wood. The chair was my mother-in-law's. She sewed and prayed in it. She was a fan of the Minnesota Twins and listened to their games in it—even when they lost.

She was sitting in her rocking chair when she died.

Cameo Bracelet

Upon graduating from Crookston High School in 1945 my parents, Pearl and Lee, gave me a cameo bracelet belonging to my grandmother, Orpha.

The bracelet is made of antique gold beads woven together by wire with a fringe on the end, and it can be made bigger or smaller. The small cameo face, possibly a Roman centurion, is set in bright gold on gold. Over the years the links have had to be rewoven.

My grandmother was born in 1842 in New York State, and died in 1897 in Crookston, Minnesota. Because I know so little about this woman, the bracelet is a real treasure to me.

I wonder when she acquired it, and who gave it to her? Did she wear it when she played the piano for a governor's daughter's wedding in Illinois?

My bracelet had a twin which my mother wore. It is believed stolen from her home.
This bracelet brings me close to my grandmother.

Important Note: Be sure to keep all of your lists, notes, and brainstormed ideas from this chapter in a separate folder. You will be using them later.

CHAPTER TWO

Writing & Writers

Introduction

Before we continue with specific kinds of writing in Chapters Three through Twelve, I want us to briefly consider some basic points about writing and writers. There are many misconceptions about writing and who "real" writers are, so I think it is important to clarify what we know and to dispel these misconceptions. I'll use the object sketch writing that you did in Chapter One as a basis for our examination of these points.

Who is a Writer?

Quite often people think that writers are some special breed of human being. We are all familiar with the stereotype of the lonely, mysterious artist struggling in his or her room, perhaps with a glass of whiskey at hand and cigarette burning in the ashtray. Of course we know that this is a caricature.

Writers are people like you and me. They come in all shapes, sizes, ages, and with often vastly different backgrounds and experiences. There is one important thing about writers, and that is *they write!*

Some people write as an occupation; let's think of them as the professionals. They might be journalists, novelists, poets, historians, or others who by education, training, and practice are skilled—often highly skilled—in what they do. Writing is their career. Other people write as an avocation, or hobby; let's think of them as the amateurs. These are people who write because they have something to say and want to share it with others, perhaps family and friends. These are people who think it's fun to play around with words and ideas.

Just as anyone with enough interest, determination, and willingness to practice can become a competent bridge player, pianist, bowler, fly fisher, or knitter, so too can anyone with enough interest and willingness to write regularly become a competent writer. The amateur might not achieve the same level of competence as the professional pianist, knitter, or writer, but that doesn't mean that he or she won't experience the same joy, excitement, and satisfaction. Who is a writer? Anyone who wants to write. You, for example, dear reader!

For Whom Do Writers Write?

People write for many reasons. It is important as you begin to write anything to consider who might read it, that is, it is important to consider your intended *audience*. This is only common sense. Let's take letter writing, for example. When you write a business letter, say, to the manufacturer of a defective product you purchased, you write quite differently than when you're writing a newsy letter to a life-long friend. And the letter to your friend is certainly different from that which you write to one of your grandchildren. That letter to your grandchild will be dramatically different from the one you write to the editor of the local newspaper in which you voice your strong opinion about some current issue in your community. All of these are examples of particular audiences. The audience for your writing is always tied to your particular purpose for writing. That's something I'll be stressing throughout the book: *purpose* and *audience.*

The audience for your writing is large and varied. Most people write for a limited number of purposes and to a limited number of people, and that's fine. One of my goals in this book, however, is to get you to also consider some other possible purposes and audiences. For example, you might want to write memoirs that you'd like to share with your family and some friends. Those same memoirs might also be shared with a wider audience through your local newspaper and magazines for Seniors. The funny stories and tall tales that you tell your grandchildren might also be turned into a children's picture book that you would then share with other children, perhaps at a local elementary school. The poetry that you write and hide away in a drawer might be submitted to a newspaper, magazine, Seniors' poetry page on the Internet, or you might self-publish a collection of your own work.

You get the idea. There are many audiences for our writing and there are many purposes. In general, I think most of us overly limit ourselves with regard to what we write and to whom. I want you to experiment as you read and work through this book. I want you to take chances. What the heck—if you're like me, you're probably too old to worry about looking silly! Who cares at this stage of our lives about looking silly?

Before we leave this brief consideration of our audience, let me highlight our first and most obvious audience: ourselves. You're your own audience; you are the first person who reads what you have written. Sometimes that's enough. Sometimes you write something because you simply want to express an emotion on paper, or you want to work out an idea, and writing helps you do that. Perhaps you want to record your daily experiences and reactions to people and events and accordingly keep a diary which no one else will read. Some people write only for themselves, and that's fine. Once again, however, I hope that after reading this book you'll also consider sharing your experiences, wit, and wisdom with a larger audience.

What Do I Write About?

Writing can be about anything. Let me repeat that: Writing can be about *anything*. Consider the object sketches we wrote. They were about ordinary things that were around our homes, things that you probably never thought of as good material for writing. You have a million things to write about. You have your whole life as source material. You have the world around you to see, smell, taste, hear, and touch and then to capture on paper. Think about all of the "firsts" in your life: first day in school, first kiss, first job, first child, first heartbreak . . . . You can write about those experiences. Remember all those people you've known in your life who were memorable: your parents, grandparents, teachers, sweethearts, childhood friends you've never seen again . . . ? Write about them. Look out your window, and what do you see? Perhaps it's the snow glittering on the branches of the maple tree; the sun setting behind the saguaro cactus and the desert ablaze; the robins on your lawn bringing with them the springtime; fireflies flashing on a warm summer night; or the birch leaves streaming golden to the ground in September—you can write about any of these.

You have a million things to write about, and you don't have to wait for "inspiration." That's another misconception or myth about writing: That people are suddenly struck by the Muse or have a flash of inspiration and then immediately capture it on paper. Sure, sometimes that happens. Sometimes an image or an idea comes to us and it is vivid and carries with it the words we want to write. But such moments are rare for all writers. Consider the professionals I mentioned above. A novelist might spend six to eight hours at the computer and only produce a page or two that she wants to keep. A poet might get an idea for a poem or might suddenly jot down an image that he wants to work with, but then he might spend days, weeks, or, even in some famous cases, years completing the poem.

You don't have to wait for inspiration, and your piece of writing doesn't have to be long, grand, noble, grammatically correct, or even spelled right. You always will be able to work with the piece, changing it by addition or deletion, fixing up the grammar, spelling, and punctuation. As I've stressed, the thing that makes writers different from non-writers is that they write.

What do you write about? Write about *particular* things. Avoid abstractions if possible. The poet William Carlos Williams always stressed that there are "no ideas but in things." It's good advice, and I try to keep it in mind as I write. Thus, don't try to write about "Love" with a capital "L." Instead, write about that flutter in your stomach you experienced with your first kiss or the way your spouse shone in your eyes on your wedding day. Here are a couple of short poems, called haiku, that I wrote as examples. Instead of writing about "Respect for All Forms of Life," I wrote:

Don't harm that ladybug
Who landed on your shoulder!
Angels come in all shapes and sizes

And instead of writing about "The Cycle of Life and Death," I wrote:

Leaves flying through the air
Streamers falling from heaven
On the way to their dark new home

You get the idea? Write about anything, but write about particular things.

When and Where Do I Write? How?

When should you write? Constantly. Anytime. Whatever time is best for you. More often is better of course than less often. I find that early mornings are best for me. Friends of mine can only write late at night or after midnight. One 90-year-old woman in one of my workshops would wake up in the middle of the night, say at 3:00 A.M., and write poems in a notebook she kept on her nightstand. She said the writing helped keep her on an "even keel," and that writing when she woke in the middle of the night kept her from worrying about things. A friend of mine carries a little notebook in his pocket and jots down ideas, words, phrases, images, and stories that he hears throughout the day. Experiment with different times and find out what works for you.

Where should you write? Again, this varies according to the individual. When at home, I prefer to write at my desk and seldom write at the kitchen table. However, when I'm away from home I work best at a kitchen table. Try different spots and see what works. Some people write best in a quiet corner of the public library. Others like to work at the dining room table after the dishes have been cleared. One man in a workshop said he could only write in our workshop and at the community center in which we met. Thus, he always arrived an hour or two before the class to work on his prose or poetry. Another woman I know will only write on her screened-in back porch, and she does this in summer and winter!

How should you write? What should you use? Once again, this will vary from person to person. I now am so used to using a computer that I find it hard to write with pen and paper. My hand begins to ache, and I seem to have a more difficult time getting going on a piece. A friend still uses her IBM electric typewriter and refuses to give it up. My brother likes yellow legal pads and blue ink, but a colleague of mine likes white legal-size paper and black ink. My wife keeps her diary on the computer. A noted poet only uses pencil for his first drafts but then goes to the typewriter for additional drafts. If you are comfortable using a particular kind of paper, pen, pencil, typewriter, or computer, stick with it and try to build a routine around it. Find out what works best for you.

Why Write?

So far in this chapter we've explored the Who, What, Where, When, and How of writing, but now we come to the most basic question of all. Why should you bother writing? Why go through all this trouble? Obviously, since you're reading this book, you already understand the value in writing. Let me mention a couple of other reasons for writing that I hope will confirm your efforts.

You have a lifetime of valuable experiences and writing about them will sharpen those memories and deepen their meanings. This is often called the "life review" process, whereby we explore again our pasts and come to understand them better and value them more. Writing also helps us discover that we often know more than we thought we did, and sometimes it opens our eyes to aspects of our own lives and to the world that we had been blind to. A noted writer once said that he didn't know what he thought until he saw it on paper. I think that's quite often true for most of us.

Writing is worth the effort because of the various purposes and audiences that you might want to address. How will your grandchildren or great-grandchildren know about your life unless you leave them something permanent, something that they can read years and years hence? How will all of that poetry bottled up inside you get expressed unless you set it down in writing? How will your indignation over some politician's thoughtless or stupid vote reach him or her and the wider community unless you publish it in the newspaper?

Lastly, writing is worth all of the effort because you will find that it's great fun. An 84-year-old woman in my present writing workshop observed, "I haven't had so much fun since I was a girl playing softball!" And her writing, with all of its humor and descriptive language, proves her excitement and joy. She knows, as I think you will also, that playing around with language, experimenting with words, unlike softball, is a game that anyone can play at any age, enjoy, and win.

Let's play!

CHAPTER THREE

Remembering Our Lives

Introduction

As our lives grow longer and our memories teem with images, events, and stories from fifty, sixty, or seventy years ago, we often begin to feel a desire, and sometimes even an urgent need, to capture our lives on paper. We often want to leave behind something of ourselves for posterity. This might be your primary purpose for reading my book. There's a kind of immortality in writing. Perhaps you like to think that a hundred years from now some distant relative will read about your childhood, your adventures as a young adult, or your life as a father or mother.

Seniors who come to my writing classes often do so because they want to tell their personal life stories. "I want to write my autobiography, from birth until now," I often hear from individuals. And I invariably reply, "Very few of our lives are, or have been, that interesting." Instead of trying to capture chronologically their experiences in autobiographies, I suggest that they begin to paint complex portraits of their lives through vivid and interesting vignettes, or brief sketches of important and memorable events in their lives. That's what I'm going to explore with you in this chapter: How to tell the story of your life through relatively short but engaging vignettes.

What Is a Vignette?

I think the best way of describing what I mean by capturing your life in vignettes and not in a chronological autobiography is by using two contrasting visual images. The first one, the chronological autobiography approach, is similar to the travel videos that people have taken on vacations and then show to friends. You know the kind I'm talking about: An hour or two of unedited videotape showing your friends arriving at their motel in Flagstaff, Arizona; then getting out of their car at the Grand Canyon; mugging for the camera; putting on their day packs; hiking down the Bright Angel Trail; taking jerky panoramic shots of the canyon walls; eating at the bottom of the canyon; and on and on. No matter how much you like your friends, and no matter how interesting they and their trip are, you know that you inevitably begin to lose attention, yawn a lot, and try to stay awake. If you weren't there, the blow-by-blow account of the trip becomes boring.

Contrast that unedited video account of a vacation with another that friends share with you. Let's consider this the vignette approach. In this instance your friends have been on the same trip to the Grand Canyon, but instead of taking video footage they have taken slides, hundreds of them. However, they don't subject you to an evening during which all of the slides are shown. (Like me, you've probably sat through such evenings, and you know how tedious they can be!) Instead, what they have done is to carefully select thirty or forty slides which highlight specific aspects of the trip. They show you what was most captivating to them, what was visually stunning, what was unusual, and what they think you might be interested in. Since they have selected a limited number of slides, your friends can talk leisurely about each one, and you can ask questions and make comments. Undoubtedly you will find this evening's presentation more engaging than the hour or so of unedited videotape.

Vignettes of your life are like those slides. Each vignette is carefully selected and written. You want to present to the reader those events and experiences—those stories of your life—that are the most captivating, stunning, and unique. You want to convey to the reader why these particular experiences are important to you and why they might be important or interesting to her or him. Therefore, in your construction of each vignette you try to be as vivid and engaging as possible. You select your words carefully and create images and dialogue that capture and hold the reader's attention. You write with an eye both to your *purpose* and to your particular *audience*.

Selecting Vignettes

What stories of your life should you tell? Out of the hundreds, if not thousands, of "slides" that you might show, which ones should you select? Of course, you probably already have many such "slides" in mind, events and stories that you want to capture in writing. Before you begin writing, however, let's work through a brainstorming and selection process that I think will be helpful to you in all of your writing. As we did in Chapter One, I'm going to ask you to follow along with me.

I'm first going to brainstorm and list some *general* topics that I might want to write about. These topics will take me into my memory, and I might recall some event, person, or time that I might want to further explore in writing. Here's a beginning list of topics:

Stories of "firsts," for example: first day in school, first date, first heartbreak, first job, and so on;

Stories of work: best job, worst job;

Stories and family expressions told by parents, grandparents, and other family members;

Stories of childhood or teenage adventures;

Stories about scary experiences, for example, a brush with death;

Stories about "forks" in your life's road;

Stories about "where you were," for example: when World War II ended, when the astronauts landed on the moon, when the millennium began on January 1, 2000, and so forth;

Stories about special places;

Stories about memorable people;

Stories about doing something or making something, for example: canoeing in the Minnesota Boundary Waters Canoe Area Wilderness, walking across the Golden Gate Bridge, giving birth to a set of twins, rebuilding the engine on your first car, and so on;

Stories about how something came to be, for example: how your relatives first came to America, how you got your name, and so forth;

Stories about funny, witty, strange, or sad conversations you overheard or in which you participated.

That's my list of brainstormed topics about which we might remember and write. Now on your sheet of paper add some more *general* topics that come to mind. Try to add at least five to ten. **Important note: Remember to keep all of your notes, lists, and brainstormed ideas from this chapter in a separate folder. You will be using them in future chapters.**

Looking Closely at One General Topic

Okay, now that you've expanded my list of general topics, let's select one and play around with it. I'm going to select the general topic of stories told by parents, grandparents, and other family members, and I'd like you to do the same. We all know those family stories that are told and re-told and passed down from generation to generation, family stories that are embroidered over time and take on the characteristics of legends or tall tales. Quite often such stories make engaging vignettes since they say something about the kind of extended family of which you are a member. Once again I'll brainstorm and list some of the stories from my family; then I'd like you to do the same. Some memorable stories are:

My grandmother's tale of the night the devil came to their cabin in Poland;

My grandfather's tale of Napoleon's gold hidden in a well in Lithuania;

My father's account of being "on the bum" during the Great Depression and having a beer in Seattle on the day Prohibition ended in 1933;

My mother's account of the ghost who came dressed in a white gown to the dancehall near the cemetery ;

My uncle's story of being wounded in Germany during WWII;

My grandfather's, father's, and now my story of the boy who accidentally shot and killed his father while deer hunting in northern Wisconsin;

My father's story of the three sisters who drowned in the Wisconsin River and whose spirits still haunt that bend in the river.

That's my list. Take some time and make a list of your own. Notice how all of my examples are of *specific* family stories. Try to brainstorm and list as many interesting family stories as you can. Again, five to ten is always a good starting point from which to choose and write.

Some Specific Things About the Family Story

Do you have a list of five or more family stories? Fine. First, let's select one particular family story we want to write about. I'm choosing the story my mother used to tell about the beautiful ghost who came to the dancehall. Select one of your stories from your brainstormed list. I know it might be hard to select only one, but that's because you probably have so many stories you'd like to write about. That's great. You certainly won't run out of ideas for a long time!

Second, let's follow the same procedure that we used in Chapter One, that is, let's brainstorm specific ideas, images, and elements of our stories by using the "Reporter's 5Ws & H": *Who, What, Where, When, Why,* and *How.* On a sheet of paper list your family story and then follow my lead in generating specific words and phrases.

My Family Story

My mother's story of the ghost who came to the dance in a white dress.

Who

My mother told the story many times. My uncle verified it as being true.

My father said he had heard about it. As an adult I read different versions of the story in collections of "urban legends."

As you're remembering who told your family story, try to recall all of the people who told it and the several variations. Of course, after many years *your* version of the story is itself one particular variation. For example, I remember my mother telling this story as a "spooky story" to us children when we were very young. We loved the thrill of being safely frightened. As my siblings and I grew older the story changed in its details, and it became more appropriate for teenagers. Then my father would sometimes tell the version of the story that he had heard from a friend who supposedly was at the same dance as my mother. At family gatherings my mother's oldest brother would swear that it was a true story. Finally, as a young adult in college I read several collections of urban legends, myths, and folklore in which I always found similar "ghost at the dance" stories. Today all of these sources are reflected, however slightly, in *my* version of my mother's story. Let's continue with our listing.

My Family Story

My mother's story of the ghost who came to the dance in a white dress.

What (happened)

A group of men on their way to a dance picked up a beautiful young woman who was standing along the highway next to the gate at the Polish National Cemetery.

Although it was autumn and chilly this particular evening, the young woman was wearing only a thin white formal gown.

The woman hardly spoke, but told the young men that she "lived nearby" the spot at which they stopped. She said her name was Lorraine.

The strange, beautiful woman was the talk of the dance. All of the men wanted a chance to dance with her.

Her skin was soft, spotless, and almost as white as her dress. She was also very cool, if not cold, to the touch even though the dancehall became very hot.

The woman asked the same young men for a ride back home.

When they approached the spot near the cemetery gate at which they picked her up, the woman told them to stop.

The young men were worried because it was 3:00 a.m., and there was no house in sight. They didn't want to leave her alone on the highway. Once again, she told them she "lived nearby."

The young men watched in awe and horror as the beautiful woman walked through the iron gate of the cemetery and disappeared.

One of the young men's uncle worked at the Chicago Tribune and he did some checking when his nephew told him the story. He found an old obituary notice for a woman named Lorraine who had been killed in a terrible automobile accident ten years earlier while she and her boyfriend were on their way to a dance in the country. She had been buried in the Polish National Cemetery in Willow Springs.

Notice how my list of *What* happened is basically the outline of the story; it's the bare bones of the plot. That's all you want to get in your brainstorming and listing: the key elements of the story from beginning to end. Look over the list of your story. Does it include a beginning? A middle? An end? Let's continue with the reporter's next question: Where?

My Family Story

My mother's story of the ghost who came to the dance in a white dress.

Where (did the story happen)

Willow Springs, Illinois—a rural area just outside the Chicago city limits; today it is a fashionable suburb.

At the time of my mother's story, it was still a largely unpopulated area.

There are several large cemeteries in the area, including the one in which my mother and father are now buried.

As I'm brainstorming ideas about my mother's story, I inevitably begin to make connections between the past and the present, that is, I connect Willow Springs as it was and as it is now and link the cemetery story that my mother told to the cemetery in which her body now lies. Writing not only helps us capture the past, but it also helps us re-create and enrich the past from our present point of view and life experiences. Let's continue.

My Family Story

My mother's story of the ghost who came to the dance in a white dress.

When (did the story happen)

My mother said she was eighteen when the ghost at the dance incident occurred. Since she was born in 1917, it must have happened in the autumn of 1935.

When you are making lists for *Where* and *When* above, try to be as specific as possible. You want your family story to become a *written* part of your family's heritage. You don't know who might be reading it fifty years from now, and he or she might be trying to place the story within a particular time frame and a particular place. If I wrote that my mother's story happened "at a dance outside Chicago when she was young," you see how vague that is. Contrast that description with this one: "When my mother was eighteen in the autumn of 1935, she went to a Saturday night dance at the Willow Springs Dance Hall. At that time Willow Springs was not simply a suburb of Chicago; instead, it was a largely unpopulated area noted for its three large cemeteries." Always keep in mind as you write: particulars, particulars, and more particulars! Let's continue with the last two of the reporter's questions.

My Family Story

My mother's story of the ghost who came to the dance in a white dress.

Why (did the story happen)

My mother said the ghost of Lorraine was lonely and wanted human contact.

My father always claimed that she was looking for her boyfriend who was drunk and driving the car when the accident occurred. He was not injured, and she wanted revenge.

In several variations of this urban legend, I read that the ghost always appeared on the evening of her death.

As we discussed in Chapter One, you have a lot of flexibility under which of the Reporter's 5Ws & H you place particular ideas, phrases, or events. For example, in my family story I perhaps could have listed my *Why* items under *What*. I also could have taken a slightly different approach and listed under *Why* the reasons my mother told us the story throughout her life. Look over the lists you have written. Do you see how particular ideas, phrases, or events might fit under one or more of the reporter's questions? You don't have to move them. I just want you to be aware of the many choices you have when you are writing most things. Let's move on to the last question: *How.*

My Family Story

My mother's story of the ghost who came to the dance in a white dress.

How (was the story told)

My mother always told the story at night. She would become very serious and lower her voice to a whisper.

At times tears would come to my mother's eyes when she reached the conclusion of the story.

As we children grew into adulthood and moved away from home, she often told the story at family gatherings, for example, during Christmas time.

It's important to try and capture in writing how different people told the family story. Fifty years from now, you and I won't be around to tell future members of our extended families how particular people told particular stories. We have to describe those tellings with words. My father told the ghost at the dance story very differently than my mother, and he was less effective in creating a mood of sadness and eeriness. When I tell the story I usually embellish it with a lot of scary details (there were red splotches of dried blood on the hem of her white dress, and so forth), and it is still much less effective than my mother's quiet telling. When you're writing about a family story, close your eyes and try to *see* and *hear* the family member as she or he actually told it.

Try a First Draft

Let's try writing a first draft of our family stories, keeping in mind what we've already explored in Chapters One and Two. We'll use our lists of *Who, What, Where, When, Why,* and *How,* but as we begin to write we will probably also discover that new words and ideas come to mind.

Once again, as I highlighted in Chapter One, I want the first sentence of my story to grab the reader's attention. Thus, I want to make it as particular and interesting as possible. I'll try three possible opening sentences to my mother's story.

> *I remember the ghost story my mother used to tell. My mother told us the story of the ghost of a young woman who appeared at a dance. When my mother was eighteen she went to a dance, and a ghost was there.*

Which of the above three sentences grabs your attention? Why? I don't like the first one that I wrote because it is too general. I'm not crazy about the second sentence because even though it is more specific—it's about a female ghost at a dance—it doesn't "flow" all that smoothly. Say the sentence out loud to yourself. Doesn't it sound cumbersome to you? It does to me, especially the part: ". . .the story of the ghost of a young woman. . . ." Saying your sentences out loud is a good way to help you see and *hear* if they are the best ones you should keep.

I like my third sentence the best: "When my mother was eighteen she went to a dance, and a ghost was there." It introduces the key elements of the story; it is particular (my mother was eighteen); and it immediately evokes a sense of mystery. The reader wants to know who the ghost was, what the ghost was doing at the dance, and how my mother was involved. I like the matter-of-fact nature of the sentence which establishes the tone of the story, that is, it is a "true" ghost story. I also like the way it sounds when I say it out loud.

Now you write at least three or more opening sentences to your family story. Play around with them the way I did with mine. Try to write a too-general or vague opening sentence, a second that perhaps is too long or awkward, and one that really "hooks" the reader into wanting to read more. Say each sentence out loud. Which one sounds the best? Which one is most specific? Select one that you like.

Since our family stories were told by someone, we have a couple of options with regard to how we might write them. I, for example, can re-tell my mother's story in my own words, trying to capture some of her tone, mood, and language. Or I can try to write it in my mother's own voice, presenting the story as best as I can remember her telling it. Here's an example of each approach.

When my mother was eighteen she went to a dance, and a ghost was there. The lovely young woman arrived by car with a group of men who had found her waiting alongside the highway near the Polish National Cemetery. She was strangely beautiful in a white formal gown, and her large dark eyes were highlighted by her pale complexion which was as white as the dress itself. "Her brown eyes were beautiful, but there was something wrong with them; they were so dull," my mother recalled.

Here's the second version in which I try to let my mother speak for herself.

"When I was eighteen I went to a dance, and a ghost was there. I remember when she got out of that old nineteen-twenty-something Ford with those three young fellas from our neighborhood," my mother began. "I wondered where they had found her. She certainly was no one that I knew. As we all walked into the Willow Springs Dance Hall, I asked Eddie, one of the fellas who had brought her, where she was from. He said they picked her up hitch-hiking in front of the Polish National Cemetery.

"That seemed odd, and she herself was odd, dressed as she was in a white formal gown while the rest of us girls simply had on our Saturday-night dresses. She was beautiful, no question about that, but in a strange kind of way. Her skin was perfectly smooth without a blemish, but it was so white, almost as white as the dress she was wearing. And her eyes! Her brown eyes were beautiful, but there was something wrong with them; they were so dull. There was no shine or sparkling to them. It was as if they were dark stone of some kind. She turned once to look at me, and I felt a chill run up my spine! I got goose bumps all over."

You see the difference in these two beginnings to my mother's ghost story? In the first I'm more or less condensing my mother's story while trying to remain true to the essential details. I use her actual words—"Her brown eyes. . . so dull"—where I think they will be most effective and to give a sense of how my mother told the story and, indeed, of my mother herself.

In the second beginning I'm letting my mother tell the story herself. Of course, I'm trying to recapture my mother's voice, and I can never do that exactly, but I'm making the best effort I can as I close my eyes and imagine her telling the story to us around the kitchen table when I was ten. Notice how the second beginning in my mother's own voice is more informal since it is in spoken English, for example, my mother always said "fellas" and not "fellows," said "sparkling to them" instead of "spark to them," and used the expression "goose bumps." Also notice how it contains more specific details than the first beginning, for example, "that old nineteen-twenty-something-Ford."

Which beginning is better? Let's not think in terms of "better" or "worse." Instead, let's think in terms of what we want to accomplish and how we can best do that. If my mother was a vivid and expressive storyteller and I can remember much of her actual language, then perhaps letting her tell the story herself is the better approach to take. If the story is one that has been handed down in your family through many storytellers and is itself a rather "bare bones," unelaborated story, then perhaps the first approach in which you re-tell the story is more appropriate. However, neither is "right" or "wrong." Both approaches can be just as effective. Your *purpose* and *audience*, of course, are important. Are you writing the story so that someone fifty years hence will not only learn the family story but will also get a sense of the person who told it, for example, in my case my mother?

Using one of your opening sentences and your lists of the 5Ws & H, try writing two openings to your family story. In the first, re-tell the story but remain true to the essential details and language of the person who told it. Also try to incorporate some of the teller's actual language—even a phrase or so. Then write a second beginning in which you let the person tell the story in her or his own words. Read both beginnings out loud to hear how they sound, and in the second especially try to capture the teller's actual *spoken* language. Give it a go!

Let's Complete a First Draft

Select one of your two openings to work with. I'm going to continue with my second in which I let my mother tell the ghost story herself. I'll refer back to my 5Ws & H lists, but as I write, other ideas, memories, or images might come to mind. Here's my continuation. You might choose to read it first or after you have worked a bit on yours.

> *"I was just out of high school myself," my mother continued. "That must have been in the fall of 1935, long before I met your dad. A whole bunch of us would drive out to the dance in Willow Springs every Saturday night. You kids have to remember that it was a lot different out there then; it wasn't just another fancy suburb of Chicago the way it is now. Naw, it was pretty lonely out there then. The three big cemeteries, a few small farms, and some houses scattered here and there were the only things out there. My gang liked it because we were far from home, or what we considered far in those days, and we could act a little wild," my mother laughed. "Some of the fellas would bring half-pints of whiskey in their suit coats, and by the end of the evening they were feelin' pretty good. Of course, I never touched any of that stuff myself," my mother grinned slyly.*

What I've done above is to continue building up the context of the story by referring back to my lists of brainstormed items. Notice how I have attempted to be *specific* so that the reader has a sense of time and place. While I was writing, other things my mother would say came to mind, for example, why she and her friends liked to go out to Willow Springs ("we could act a little wild") and the fact that drinking was often involved. I continue to use my mother's spoken language, for example, "Naw" instead of "No," "fellas," and "feelin'" instead of "feeling." Notice too how I try to give the reader indirectly a glimpse of my mother's personality when I say she laughed about being "a little wild" and "grinned slyly" when she said she never drank any of the liquor.

Look at your own family story up to this point in time. Would a reader fifty years from now have a clear sense of a particular person telling a story in a particular time and place? Would the reader get a glimpse of the uniqueness of the person telling the story by the language that's being used or by how you are describing the person? Read what you have written out loud once again. Then close your eyes and try to see and hear the person telling the story. Have you captured in the best way you can what the person said and how he or she said it? Let's go on with our stories.

"Once the band started playing, the fellas wanted to dance with the beautiful pale stranger. Us girls of course were a bit jealous, but all of the boys came back to us after they had only one dance with her. Not a single fella asked her to dance a second time. A boy, Frank, that I had sort of a crush on at the time told me her name was Lorraine, and while we danced he said, 'She don't talk very much.'" My mother looked up at us as we sat around the dimly lit kitchen table.

She held out her hands and began to wring them as if trying to bring feeling back into them. "And then I remember Frank hugging me even tighter as we danced and squeezing my hands. 'You feel so good and warm, Helen,' he said, 'not like that Lorraine. She feels like ice.'"

Notice again how I'm using my mother's speaking voice—"fella," "Us girls," "I had sort of a crush on"—and specific *visual* images that I recall as I write. That is, my mother wringing her hands as if they were very cold, and the man with whom she was dancing holding her tight to feel the warmth of her body. These images not only add to the mystery of the story, but they also show how my mother used certain dramatic gestures and images to tell the story to us. Look over your draft now. Does it contain any specific visual images that will help make the story come alive? If so, fine. If not, is there one that you might add to what you now have on paper? Give it a go! And then let's continue with our stories.

"By the end of the dance all of the boys there had danced once with Lorraine, and she was then left sitting like a beautiful wall flower next to the bandstand. I remember thinking that she looked like one of those unnatural flowers that you see in a hot house, you know, an orchid or something like it from some tropical country that you get for a school dance and keep alive in the ice box. Unnatural. Several girls sat down next to her and tried to talk with her, but she didn't say much, just 'Yes' and 'No.' So we left her alone. The funny thing is that she didn't seem to mind just sitting there alone. She had this crooked smile on her face, and she followed the dancers with those dark eyes of hers."

I'll point out, yet again, as we continue writing how I try to capture my mother's voice by using words that were common during her youth but are seldom used today: "hot house" for greenhouse, and "ice box" for refrigerator.

> *"The dance ended at 2:00 a.m., and we all piled into cars to head back to Chicago. Some of the fellas were pretty drunk and shouldn't of been driving. Lorraine simply walked up to the boys that had picked her up and waited for them to offer a ride. It was pretty cold out at that time of night, but she didn't have a coat on or sweater or anything, just that thin white dress. We left for the city in a line of cars, oh, there must have been twenty or more. The car I was in was right behind Lorraine's. We all went slowly because of the boys' drinking and because the highway was very dark—there were no lights like today.*
>
> *"When we approached one of the side gates to the Polish National Cemetery, I saw the car in front pull over to the shoulder. We pulled over behind them, thinking they might be having car trouble or something. In our headlights we saw the boys talking and gesturing to Lorraine inside the car, and then we saw one of them open the back door, and she got out." My mother stared over our heads, her eyes wide, as if she were seeing something wonderful or frightening again. She whispered without looking at us, "And then in those bright headlights in that black, starless night we watched Lorraine walk through the iron bars of the cemetery fence and disappear."*

This is one version of my mother's story. Sometimes she would tell it with her actually seeing Lorraine walk through the cemetery gate, and at other times she would tell the story with her only *hearing* about the disappearance. I've chosen this version to write because I think it is the most dramatic. Let's bring our family stories to a conclusion.

"Yes, she was a ghost all right. One of the boys in our bunch had an uncle who worked for the Trib in the newsroom. When he told his uncle what had happened, the uncle laughed, but then he went back and checked through old copies of the newspaper. Do you know what he found?"

"My mother looked at each one of us sitting around the table and waited for us to answer, but none of us did. We were too awe-struck. "He found that ten years earlier, on the exact same evening, a young woman named Lorraine Tomazak was killed in a terrible automobile accident while on her way to a dance at the Willow Springs Dance Hall. The boy she was with was drunk and ran off the road and smashed head-on into a tree. She went through the windshield and was killed instantly, but he only suffered minor cuts and bruises. They buried her at the Polish National Cemetery."

"My mother bowed her head and rubbed her eyes. "Why did she leave her grave and appear at the dance? Some said that she was looking for the fella who killed her, that she wanted revenge. I don't believe that, no, not at all. I think she came back because she was lonely. Can you imagine what it must be like to be locked in a coffin and buried six feet under the cold, damp ground?" We all imagined it and shuddered. "Can you imagine how alone she was, longing to be alive again, to be with young people, to laugh, and to dance?" Tears welled in my mother's eyes and ran down her cheeks. "I believe that Lorraine came back that evening because she simply wanted to be held in someone's arms. She simply wanted to feel once again the warmth of living persons

before she had to return forever to the darkness and aloneness of her grave."

Looking Again at Our First Drafts

Now that we have a draft of our family stories we can go back and look at them with an eye to making improvements. Just as we did in Chapter One, we'll look at what we might *take out* of our family stories because the words, phrases, or sentences don't really add much to the story or because they are redundant. Then we'll look to see what we might *add* to make our story more vivid and descriptive. Since these family stories were told by particular people, we'll also see if we've captured the *speaking voice* of the person telling the story and if we've presented a *portrait of the person* as he or she told the story. Here's my complete family story as told by my mother. I'll just give examples of each of these revision strategies. I've numbered each one.

"When I was eighteen I went to a dance, and a ghost was there. I remember when she got out of that old nineteen-twenty-something Ford with those three young fellas from our neighborhood," my mother began. "I wondered where they had found her. She certainly was no one that I knew. As we all walked into the Willow Springs Dance Hall, I asked (1) ~~Eddie,~~ one of the fellas who had brought her, where she was from. He said they picked her up hitch-hiking in front of the Polish National Cemetery.

"That seemed odd, and she herself was odd, dressed as she was in a white formal gown while the rest of us girls simply

had on our Saturday-night dresses. She was beautiful, no question about that, but in a strange kind of way. Her skin was perfectly smooth without a blemish, but it was so white, almost as white as the dress she was wearing. And her eyes! Her brown eyes were beautiful, but there was something wrong with them; they were so dull. There was no shine or sparkling to them. It was as if they were dark stone of some kind. She turned once to look at me, and I felt a chill run up my spine! I got goose bumps all over,"(2) **my mother said shaking her shoulders and rubbing her arms as if she were shivering.**

"I was just out of high school myself," my mother continued. "That must have been in the fall of 1935, long before I met your dad. A whole bunch of us would drive out to the dance in Willow Springs every Saturday night. You kids have to remember that it was a lot different out there then; it wasn't just another fancy suburb of Chicago the way it is now. Naw, it was pretty lonely out there then. The three big cemeteries, a few small farms, and some houses scattered here and there were the only things out there. My bunch liked it because we were far from home, or what we considered far in those days, and we could act a little wild," my mother laughed. "Some of the fellas would bring half-pints of ~~whiskey~~ *(2)* **Jim Beam** *in their suit coats, and by the end of the evening they were feelin' pretty good. Of course, I never touched any of that stuff myself," my mother grinned slyly.*

"Once the band started playing, the fellas wanted to dance with the beautiful **(1)** ~~pale~~ *stranger. Us girls of course were a bit jealous, but all of the boys came back to us after they had only one dance with her. Not a single fella asked her to dance a second time. A boy, Frank, that I had sort of a crush on at the time told me her name was Lorraine, and*

while we danced he said, 'She don't talk very much.'" My mother looked up at us as we sat around the dimly-lit kitchen table. She held out her hands and began to wring them as if trying to bring feeling back into them. "And then I remember Frank hugging me even tighter as we danced and squeezing my hands. 'You feel so good and warm, Helen,' he said, 'not like that Lorraine. She feels like ice.'

"By the end of the dance all of the boys there had danced once with Lorraine, and she was then left sitting like a beautiful wall flower next to the bandstand. I remember thinking that she looked like one of those unnatural flowers that you see in a hot house, you know, an orchid (3) ~~or something like it from some tropical country~~ that you get for a school dance and keep alive in the ice box. Unnatural. Several girls sat down next to her and tried to talk with her, but she didn't say much, just 'Yes' and 'No.' So we left her alone. The funny thing is that she didn't seem to mind just sitting there alone. She had this crooked smile on her face, and she followed the dancers with those dark eyes of hers.

*"The dance ended at 2:00 A.M., and we all piled into cars to head back to Chicago. Some of the fellas were pretty drunk and shouldn't have been driving. (4) **If I knew then what I know now, I certainly wouldn't have gotten into a car with any driver who had been drinking.** Lorraine simply walked up to the boys that had picked her up and waited for them to offer a ride. It was pretty cold out at that time of night, but she didn't have a coat on or sweater or anything, just that thin white dress. We left for the city in a line of cars, oh, there must have been twenty or more. The car I was in was right behind Lorraine's. We all went slowly because of the boys' drinking and because the highway was very dark—there were no lights like today.*

"*When we approached one of the side gates to the Polish National Cemetery, I saw the car in front pull over to the shoulder. We pulled over behind them, thinking they might be having car trouble or something. In our headlights we saw the boys talking and gesturing to Lorraine inside the car, and then we saw one of them open the back door, and she got out.*"

My mother stared over our heads, her eyes wide, as if she were seeing something wonderful or frightening again. She whispered without looking at us, "*And then in those bright headlights in that black, starless night we watched Lorraine walk through the iron bars of the cemetery fence and disappear.*

"*(1) ~~Yes, she was a ghost all right.~~ One of the boys in our bunch had an uncle who worked for the Trib in the newsroom. When he told his uncle what had happened, the uncle laughed, but then he went back and checked through old copies of the newspaper. Do you know what he found?*"

My mother looked at each one of us sitting around the table and waited for us to answer, but none of us did. (1) ~~*We were too awe-struck.*~~ "*He found that ten years earlier, on the exact same evening, a young woman named Lorraine Tomazak was killed in a terrible automobile accident while on her way to a dance at the Willow Springs Dance Hall. The boy she was with was drunk and ran off the road and smashed head-on into a tree. She went through the windshield and was killed instantly, but he only suffered minor cuts and bruises. They buried her at the Polish National Cemetery.*

(4) ~~My mother bowed her head and rubbed her eyes.~~ "*Why did she leave her grave and appear at the dance? Some said that she was looking for the fella who killed her, that she wanted revenge. I don't believe that, no,*

not at all. I think she came back because she was lonely. Can you imagine what it must be like to be locked in a coffin and buried six feet under the cold, damp ground?" We all imagined it and shuddered. "Can you imagine how alone she was, longing to be alive again, to be with young people, to laugh, and to dance?"

*(4) **My mother bowed her head.** Tears welled in her ~~my mother's~~ eyes and ran down her cheeks. "I believe that Lorraine came back that evening because she simply wanted to be held in someone's arms. She simply wanted to feel once again the warmth of living persons before she had to return forever to the darkness and aloneness of her grave."*

The first thing I've done is to read through my draft and see what I might *take out.* That's probably the first thing you should do when you're working with a first draft of your writing. Most writers typically write more than needed when they're first getting their ideas down on paper. That's why professional writers, for example, novelists, will often delete a third or a half of a manuscript once they start to do a second draft. I've labeled as *(1)* the things that I'm going to take out. I'll briefly discuss why.

*As we all walked into the Willow Springs Dance Hall, I asked (1) **Eddie**, one of the fellas who had brought her, where she was from.*

While I continue to stress that specificity is important in your writing, I don't think the name "Eddie" is important here. He is never mentioned again in my mother's story. Thus, I think the sentence is better without the personal name: "As we walked into the Willow Springs Dance Hall, I asked one of the fellas who had brought her where she was from."

> *"Once the band started playing, the fellas wanted to dance with the beautiful **(1) pale** stranger.*

I had already written that Lorraine was almost as white as the dress she was wearing. Thus, adding "pale" here seems to be redundant. It's probably just my natural inclination—an inclination that you too might have—to use a lot of adjectives, even when they're not needed. This sentence now reads: "Once the band started playing, the fellas wanted to dance with the beautiful stranger."

> *"(1) Yes, she was a ghost all right.*

I deleted this entire sentence because it belabors the obvious. My mother was telling us a ghost story, and by this point in the tale we all knew that Lorraine was a ghost. Why say it again?

> *(1) We were too awe-struck.*

I took out this sentence because it's simply not true. As children we might have been amazed or scared, but we weren't "awe-struck." I was probably trying for some kind of "literary effect" here, and it doesn't work.

Now why don't you read through your first draft and see where you might be able to *take out* at least a couple of words, phrases, or even sentences. Don't be afraid to cut! It's better to have a lean piece of writing than a bloated one.

The next thing I've done is to see where I might be able to *add* to the story in order to make it more effective. I've labeled these additions *(2)*.

> *I got goose bumps all over,"* *(2)* **my mother said shaking her shoulders and rubbing her arms as if she were shivering.**

I've added this description of my mother's actions because I wanted to capture *how* she told the story to us kids as we sat around the kitchen table in the evening.

> *Some of the fellas would bring half-pints of* ~~*whiskey*~~ *(2) **Jim Beam** in their suit coats, and by the end of the evening they were feelin' pretty good.*

Here I've changed the general term, "whiskey," for the specific kind of whiskey, "Jim Beam." I did this because I think the reader can better picture the half-pint bottles by name (if he or she knows different kinds of whiskeys, of course) and because, as I remembered, that's what my mother actually said. The sentence now reads: "Some of the fellas would bring half-pints of Jim Beam in their suit coats, and by the end of the evening they were feelin' pretty good."

You try it now. See if there's anything you might add to your first draft to make it stronger.

The third thing I've done is to look over my draft and see and hear where I'm capturing the *speaking voice* of my mother and where I'm not. Of course, only I know that, and you'll have to take my word that my one change is appropriate. I've labeled this change *(3)*.

I remember thinking that she looked like one of those unnatural flowers that you see in a hot house, you know, an orchid **(3)** ~~or something like it from some tropical country~~ *that you get for a school dance and keep alive in the ice box.*

My mother would not say "or something like it from some tropical country." That's something I added because I thought it might sound good. The sentence now reads: "I remember thinking that she looked like one of those unnatural flowers that you see in a hot house, you know, an orchid that you get for a school dance and keep alive in the ice box."

Look through your family story and see where you try to capture the speaker's actual voice. Say those parts out loud. Is that the way the speaker would actually say it? Close your eyes and say those parts out loud. Can you see and hear the speaker? If you think you can make any changes to actually capture the speaker's voice, do so now.

The last thing I've done is to re-read the story to see if there's anything I might add which would give the reader a more *complete portrait* of my mother, that is, the kind of person she was as seen through her storytelling. I've labeled two such additions as *(4)*.

(4) If I knew then what I know now, I certainly wouldn't have gotten into a car with any driver who had been drinking.

I added this sentence because even though my mother alluded to the fact that she also did some drinking at the dance and was a "little wild," she was concerned that we did not do the same. This is the kind of indirect "motherly advice" she would often give us.

> *(4) My mother bowed her head and rubbed her eyes.*
> *(4) My mother bowed her head.* Tears welled in her ~~my mother's~~ eyes and ran down her cheeks.

Notice what I've done here. I've taken the sentence "My mother bowed her head and rubbed her eyes" and moved it down to the next paragraph in which I show the emotional impact that the story had on my mother. I think it is now more effective. The sentence now reads: "My mother bowed her head. Tears welled in her eyes and ran down her cheek."

See if there is any place in your draft where you might add or move something in order to give the reader a fuller, richer, portrait of the person telling the story.

Review of What We've Done

In this chapter we've begun to do what many Seniors want to do with their writing, and that is capture their pasts. We explored the importance of writing interesting *vignettes* instead of blow-by-blow chronological accounts of our lives. Second, we brainstormed a general list of topics about which we might write. We considered stories of our "firsts," stories of memorable places and events, stories of work, and so forth. From this general list we selected one topic: family stories that are told and retold among members of a family. Third, we then brainstormed a list of such family stories and selected one that we'd like to capture in writing.

Once we selected the family story we wanted to write we followed the same "Reporter's 5Ws & H" format that we did in Chapter One; we made lists of words, phrases, and ideas under the headings *Who, What, Where, When, Why* and *How*. Then we considered our opening sentence and how we might shape it in order to grab the reader's attention.

As we began to write our family stories we saw that we had a couple of options. We could either re-tell the story in our own words as we remember a particular person telling it, adding where appropriate particular things that the person might have said, or we could allow the speaker to tell her or his own story. In this second choice we would pay special attention to the speaker's actual voice as best as we could remember it. I chose the second option for my story.

Once we had a first draft we went back and worked on revising it where appropriate. We considered four kinds of possible revision: taking something out of the text; adding something to it; capturing the speaking voice of the person who told the story; and shaping a portrait of the person through his or her telling of the story.

This was a long chapter, but you now have an interesting family story, a vignette, that you feel good about and will want to share with others. Hopefully you are also more comfortable with the process that we'll follow throughout the book. Let's move on to Chapter Four now and continue writing vignettes about our pasts.

Writing about Memorable People

Introduction

Our lives are made up of stories which we tell and re-tell and which are told by others. In the last chapter we wrote about family stories that continue to impact us in some way. I wrote about a ghost story my mother used to tell and in doing so I made connections to the past and possibly to the future when I am no longer around; however, I also indirectly sketched a brief portrait of my mother. Our focus in this chapter will be upon the people in our lives who not only told stories that we want to remember and capture in print for posterity, but also upon people who in various ways have helped to shape us.

As we explored in Chapter Three, it is most often through vignettes that we are able to capture the essence of things.

These "slides" or snapshots allow us to focus on particulars and help us avoid writing in generalities. This especially holds true when we are writing about special people in our lives. Vignettes allow us to *show* a person's unique characteristics, say, her selfless generosity, rather than simply *telling* about it. For example, writing that my mother "was a kind and generous woman" doesn't really give you any idea of who she was. I could write the same thing about any number of people. If, however, I wrote a vignette about the rich, crumbly, egg-butter-condensed milk-homemade bread my mother used to bake and take over to the lonely and poor widowers in the neighborhood, you'd get some insight into her personality.

Vignettes about memorable people in our lives honor the memory of those individuals. I have found in my workshops with Seniors that almost all writers want to capture in print those people who made a significant impact in their lives. Quite often a writer will create many vignettes about a particular person, *showing* him in all of his complexity. One woman, for example, wrote fifteen or more vignettes about her father, and in doing so she created a collage-like portrait of him from when she was a child until his death when she was middle-aged. Before we begin writing our own vignettes about memorable people, let's read a moving portrait of a hired man written by Dan Kiernan, a fine writer in my present writing group.

Oney

He worked as hired man for my grandfather when he was a young man. He worked for us and our farm neighbors, the Tracys and the Welches when he was an old man.

His Christian name was Owen O'Keefe, but everyone called him "Oney."

When at our place he always had time to play checkers no matter how tired he was at night. He helped me make my first slingshot and talked to me like I was grown up.

I can see him asleep in the rocker on the porch, gaunt, his gray head close to the newspaper he had been reading. He had black eyebrows and clear blue eyes and always kept his bib overalls and blue work shirt very clean.

He was one of the many single men my mother called "his own worst enemy." He had what the Irish call "A love for the liquor."

We could always tell when the ache was on him. He grew quiet, and I could hear him pace the floor in the room next to mine. Before dawn I could hear his step going downstairs and out into the road toward town.

He was the older of two brothers with no girls in the family. His brother, Pat, was sent to live with an uncle so he could go to school in St. Paul. He became very successful selling Catholic life insurance but seldom visited Oney. Pat was never spoken ill of by Oney, and he seemed proud that his brother had "made something of himself."

As elder son, Oney had to take care of his parents and farm their 220 acres. His father died of consumption when Oney was in his early twenties, and his mother died a few years later of cancer. All but 40 acres and a one-room shack was left after expenses.

I worried about him in winter. In the shack my mother called "a disgrace" was an old wood cook stove, a table, one broken chair, and a barrel that served many purposes. His bed was covered by an old cowhide without pillows or sheets. He had several cans of pork & beans on the window sill and would open and heat one in a pan of hot water. He didn't eat much when he was drinking.

Sometimes we found him asleep in the barn when he couldn't make it home from town. He was proud enough to refuse to come inside to eat until I begged him.

Oney was gentle with the livestock and with people. I never heard him use a profane word. He was respectful and shy with women.

He died while living with the Little Sisters of the Poor. He had given his farm to his nephews. He was a decent man, his own worst enemy, and my friend.

This beautiful tribute to a seemingly insignificant farm laborer helps keep Oney alive in the minds, and I believe also the hearts, of all those who read it. Dan has given Oney a kind of immortality through his short sketch. Notice how brief this vignette is but also how powerful. As I already have remarked, our writing does not have to be long. Less is usually more. Notice also how Dan has used several aspects of writing which we have discussed in Chapters One, Two, and Three. His *opening sentences* immediately grab our attention and place Oney in a multigenerational context. The *particulars* that Dan uses give us a quick, but deep, portrait of Oney: He was willing to play checkers with the boy even though he was tired, and he talked to him like a grown up; he was gentle with livestock and people; he never used a profane word. Dan also uses a unique *vernacular expression* to describe Oney's craving of liquor: the "ache was on him." And, lastly, he *ends* this vignette *with a strong sentence*: "He was a decent man, his own worst enemy, and my friend." This vignette not only tells us about Oney, but about Dan as well.

Selecting a Memorable Person About Whom to Write

I'm sure that you can think of many people in your life about whom you would like to write; nevertheless, let's stick to the format we've been using and brainstorm a list of possibilities. Thinking chronologically often helps us remember important people we might have forgotten. I'll get you started:

People from our earliest years: parents; grandparents; siblings; other relatives; neighbors who cared for us—I remember my aunt in the next apartment who babysat us; children with whom we played;

People from our childhood: teachers—I remember Sister Mary Jean Frances from St. Bridget's School; neighborhood or town role models—I remember Mrs. Labney, the honest and kind owner of the local grocery store; school friends; adults with whom we might have worked—I remember the old man I used to help with his garden; people with whom we had brief, but memorable, encounters—I remember the old Black man who used to come through the alleys with his horse and wagon crying "Rags-a-lie!";

People from our young adulthood: high school friends and first loves—I remember dark-haired Carolyn and then tall and blond Barbara in high school; people with whom we worked on a variety of jobs; pastors, ministers, rabbis, and other members of the clergy who might have counseled us;

People after we left home and were on our own: those in the military—I remember Corporal Carleton from boot camp; friends and teachers at college; colleagues at our first long-term jobs; our future spouse; our own children;

People from our middle years: friends that have remained friends for decades; new acquaintances; important people from our communities; individuals who have caused us to make dramatic changes in the directions of our lives—I remember a professor who said I should pursue an advanced degree;

     People from our later years: new friends that we've made, perhaps since we've retired; grandchildren; individuals we've encountered with new interests—I remember Bertha Bess who joined one of my Senior writing groups in southern Illinois.

That's a list of ideas to get you started. Now you make a list of memorable people from different periods of your life about whom you think you'd like to write vignettes. **Important Note: Be sure to keep all of your lists, notes, and brainstormed ideas from this chapter in a separate folder. You will be using them in a future chapter.**

Above I was, for the most part, brainstorming general categories of people. As you make your list, try to be *specific;* list particular people. For example, I mentioned Sister Mary Jean Frances, my fifth grade teacher; Mrs. Labney, the woman who owned the next door grocery store; Bertha Bess, the feisty septuagenarian who wrote funny poetry; and the love of my sophomore year in high school, Barbara.

Looking Closely at One Memorable Person

I'm going to do something a little different in this chapter; I'm going to use actual vignettes about memorable people that Seniors in my classes have written. I'll first select four that I think are especially engaging. They are about:

A father

A neighbor who developed Alzheimer's disease

An elderly aunt

A childhood sweetheart who turned up sixty years later

Any one of the four would serve first as a good model, but I'm going to begin with the vignette that John Peterson wrote about his father. He titled it "My Papa." Then we'll read Della Baker's about her aunt.

From your list of particularly memorable people, select three or four that you first want to think and write about. Put them on a separate list as I have done above. Then from that group of three or four pick the person you want to begin writing about now.

Some Specific Things About the Memorable Person

Let's begin by once again using the Reporter's 5Ws & H to organize our thoughts: *Who, What, Where, When, Why,* and *How*. On a sheet of paper, follow along as I use John's vignette about his father as a model.

John's Memorable Person
Papa

Who
Shoe salesman
Family man
Tolerant of others
Gentleman

As you're listing things about your memorable person, be sure to include both concrete aspects, for example, John's father was a shoe salesman, and other more personal or psychological characteristics, for example, John's father was tolerant and a gentleman.

John's Memorable Person
Papa

What (was special):
Worked long hours six days a week
Walked home for lunch
Never owned a car
Chewed Right Cut Tobacco
Played the Gulbranson piano
Had a sense of humor

In your listing of what was special or unique about your memorable person are you including *specific* things? Remember good writing tries to include *particulars*. Notice in my listing for John's father I'm not just writing "chewed tobacco" or "played the piano"; instead I'm writing "Right Cut Tobacco" and the "Gulbranson piano." I'll quote from the doctor-poet William Carlos Williams once again: "No ideas but in things."

John's Memorable Person
Papa

Where (did this vignette occur)
Leader Store
Buffalo, Minnesota
Home up the hill from the store
Evening dinner table

John's vignette about his father, as you will see, is very localized, very particular. It moves from the store in which he worked as a clerk to their home up the hill from the store.

John's Memorable Person
Papa

When
Great Depression
Hot summer day
One particular afternoon
Later that particular evening

Sometimes when we are writing vignettes about particular people we even remember specific times and dates. I once wrote a sketch about two memorable people from my youth, the Everly Brothers, and how we were in Marine Corps Boot Camp together in San Diego. I recalled how we "boots" all gathered on Christmas Eve 1961 and listened, teary-eyed, to the two shaven-headed brothers sing "Silent Night."

John's Memorable Person
Papa

Why
Father greeted all women
Mother was strait-laced, even jealous
John misunderstood father's remark to cute new employee
Mother fumed

I've already remarked above that the 5Ws & H give us a lot of room in which to play with ideas. Items that we put under one category might just as easily be placed in another. The important thing about the 5Ws & H is that they give us a way to organize our ideas. Thus, in this particular example, I'm using *Why* to list the central action or conflict in John's vignette. As you will see, the misunderstanding allows John to sketch a brief portrait of his father; at the same time, however, he also gives us a glimpse into his mother's personality.

John's Memorable Person
Papa

How
Mother was silent
Refused to kiss father
Father was confused
Mother bursts into "That girl! Morning Cheer!"
Father clarifies misunderstanding
Family all laugh

I'm using *How* here to indicate how the conflict in this story was resolved. Depending upon the vignette you're thinking about and are going to write your *How* might be different.

Try a First Draft

Since John's vignette about his father is already complete, I'll simply highlight certain aspects that I think are well-done and which might give you ideas as you compose your story of a memorable person. Let's begin with our *opening sentence or sentences* which will grab the reader's attention. Here's John's:

> *We lacked many things during the Depression years, but there were always a lot of pencils and shoe horns around our house.*

John is an especially witty writer. Notice how his opening sentence immediately makes us wonder why there were a lot of pencils and, of all things, shoe horns around the house. His second sentence gives us the answer:

Papa was a shoe salesman.

Look over your list of 5Ws & H and try at least three different opening sentences. Try writing one, such as John's, that makes the reader ask him- or herself a *question*. Try another opening sentence that begins with a *statement of fact*. For example, John could have began this piece with "Papa was a shoe salesman." Then try a third opening which is *humorous*. For example, "Papa laughed and said he played 'This Little Piggy Went to Market' for a living. He was a shoe salesman." After you have a few opening sentences, select one that you like and which captures the mood you want to capture in your vignette.

Since you are writing a vignette about a memorable person, you want to include specific and significant things that will give the reader some insight into that person. They do not have to be "grand" or necessarily unusual things. Most of us don't live grand or unusual lives. The lives we do live, however, are interesting in themselves if we only take time to notice them. Here's the way John begins to paint a portrait of his father as a hard-working, tolerant, and considerate family man, the kind of person that I think most of us would like to know.

We lacked many things during the Depression years, but there were always a lot of pencils and shoe horns around our house. Papa was a shoe salesman. He worked long hours six days a week at the old Leader Store in Buffalo. He never owned a car. At noon he walked up the hill for dinner laden with groceries and the news of the day. When someone died my mother would ask, "Was he a Christian?" My father, a tolerant man, would say, "Well, he was a good Lutheran, Catholic, Methodist, or whatever."

When Papa came in the door my two sisters and I would beg him for treats until two regular treat days were arranged. On Wednesdays we got a five-stick pack of Wrigley's Juicy Fruit Gum. Each child received a stick. Mama got a stick. Papa chewed Right Cut Tobacco so we kids divided the remaining stick in thirds. But Saturday was the best treat day when we got Milky Way candy bars!

Notice how John is *showing* us, not telling us, something about his father's character and, indirectly, about his whole family through the use of simple *dialogue* ("Was he a Christian?"), *example* ("we kids divided the remaining stick in thirds"), and *specifics* ("laden with groceries and news of the day"; "Wrigley's Juicy Fruit Gum"; "Milky Way candy bars").

Using your 5Ws & H list, your opening sentence(s), and other ideas and images that come to mind as you begin to write, try at least two paragraphs that begin to sketch a portrait of your memorable person. Remember: showing not telling; relevant particulars or details; perhaps examples; and perhaps dialogue. Take your time. There's no rush.

John continues in his vignette to draw a portrait of his father. We begin to get a more rounded image of the man.

Papa enjoyed an occasional cigar which he smoked for the house plants so as not to set a bad example for me. He said he chewed tobacco to preserve his teeth and would quit when he got dentures, which he did.

> *A store clerk's salary didn't go far, but Papa managed to buy a new Gulbranson piano with three pedals on the installment plan. The third pedal didn't do anything but served as a status symbol. In the evenings we would gather around the piano and sing, and Papa would play the mandolin.*

Notice the humor in "Papa enjoyed an occasional cigar which he smoked for the house plants so as not to set a bad example for me." We can picture the man sitting there in the evening and saying this to his son as he points to the potted plants. This "white lie" is balanced by the fact that John's father *did* quit chewing tobacco once he got his false teeth. Lastly, we continue to get a portrait of the family as a whole as we see them singing around the piano in the evening.

Continue to develop your vignette by writing at least one more or perhaps two additional paragraphs. They don't have to be long.

In order to be interesting to the reader, almost all stories need to have some sort of *conflict or problem* which helps drive the plot, or action of the story. Since vignettes of people are little stories, they too work best when we get a picture of a person as he or she is dealing or struggling with some problem. We *see* the person's character and are not simply told about it. Here's John's next paragraph:

> *A true gentleman, he always tipped his hat at every lady we met on our Sunday afternoon strolls around town.*

"Who was she?" Mama would ask. Papa would reply, "Some customer."

This is a transitional paragraph in John's story. Notice how he is still describing his father—he always tipped his hat to the ladies—but at the same time is introducing a potential problem. We can see from his mother's question—"Who was she?"—that she might have a jealous side to her.

Look at what you've written up to this point in time. Consider your opening sentence(s). Will your opening grab the reader's interest? Look at how you've developed a sketch of the person. Are you showing the person through particular details, examples, and, perhaps, dialogue? Is there a conflict or problem in your portrait which helps show the person's character or uniqueness? If you've already established a particular conflict or problem in your vignette, further develop it in another paragraph. If you haven't introduced the problem, then do so in a transitional paragraph. Be sure to look at your list of 5Ws & H, any other notes you might have added by now, and John's example. Give it a go!

Here's the rest of John's vignette of his father. Notice how he quickly develops the conflict through misunderstanding, describes his mother's jealous reaction, and then resolves the problem through his father's explanation. Since John loves to play with words and humor, notice also how he brings his story to a conclusion by using the expression "regular grind."

One day Mama sent me to the store for something, and I noticed a cute new girl in the grocery department. Papa called her "Morning Cheer!"

When I returned home I shared this joyful news with my strait-laced mother. "Guess what? Papa calls that cute new girl down at the store 'Morning Cheer!'"

Few words were exchanged the rest of the afternoon. Mama prepared the evening meal in silence. When Papa came home there was no welcome kiss from Mama. Puzzled, "What's wrong?" he asked.

"YOU—you and that girl—MORNING CHEER! THAT GIRL!"

"Oh, that Morning Cheer," Papa replied laughing, "'Morning Cheer' is a new coffee, and that girl is always promoting it; so everyone calls her 'Morning Cheer'!"

Then we all had a good laugh and sat down to supper, but for a few hours that hot long summer afternoon love was a regular grind at our house!

Although this is primarily a sketch of his father, John has also given us a glimpse into his mother's personality and into his own naivete as a child. It's a warm-hearted story that honors his father and shows the love between his father and mother and among all the members of the family.

Take your time and further develop your character vignette through particulars, examples, dialogue, specific actions, and the resolution of the conflict or problem that is driving your story. Just as we want to open a piece with an attention-getting sentence, we want to close it with a strong paragraph. Whether your story is as lighthearted as John's or more serious as Dan's sketch of Oney, work on an ending that will stay in the reader's mind. Do not rush the rest of your memorable character vignette. Good writing takes time.

Looking Again at Our First Drafts

Since this is John's story and not mine, I will not attempt to revise it. Any piece, I repeat, any piece can be revised. I know John worked on this vignette for some time. The important thing with most writing that we want to save, share with others, and perhaps pass down to future generations is that we at the very least give it a second look, that we "re-vision" it. We might not make many or even any changes, but I think that some tinkering with a piece will help to make it stronger, more vivid, and more memorable.

Re-read out loud your complete memorable character vignette. How does it *sound?* Are there places where it sounds awkward and doesn't flow especially well? If you included *dialogue,* does it sound natural and the way the person or persons would have spoken? Are there any words, phrases, or sentences that you might *add* to make the story stronger or clearer? Is there anything you might *delete* because it is redundant, irrelevant, or simply uninteresting? Have you used or considered using *vernacular expressions* (such as John's "regular grind") which might make your story more lively? Lastly, are you *showing, not telling,* the person about whom you're writing?

Consider all of these aspects and then make at least two changes to your first draft. Of course, you might make more, but the important thing is to get into the habit of working with a draft and not simply going with what you've first written. Give it a try.

Writing About a Second Memorable Person

Now that you've got the hang of it, why don't you write a second vignette about a memorable person in your life.

Go back to the lists you brainstormed and select another person. Then follow the same procedure we went through for the first vignette. Take your time and don't rush things. Have fun! You might work on this second sketch over a couple of days if you choose, but try to include the following: brainstorm; make lists on paper; use the 5Ws & H; create a strong opening; utilize particulars, examples, and dialogue; develop a conflict and resolution; close with a strong ending; and look again at your work after you have a first draft. Here's a second example which illustrates some of the things we've been exploring, especially the use of dialogue. It's shorter than John's, but it is also humorous. It's by another Senior writer, and is about her aunt.

Aunty

I was raised by my father's older sister. She was a piano teacher, giving lessons both at her home and her pupils' homes. Aunty loved what she did, and was at it after her 65th birthday.

When coming home from one of these lessons, she dashed around the front of the streetcar and was knocked down by a car. Now Aunty weighed about 90 pounds soaking wet. She would go from here to there in a straight line at about 100 miles an hour.

That afternoon as I sat trying to make some sort of sense out of my homework assignment, the phone rang. When I answered it a female voice said, "Now, don't worry, everything is all right. Your aunt was hit by a car. We can't send her home until she stops wandering."

I asked what she meant by "wandering." The nurse said, "She keeps insisting that she be allowed to go home because her mother will be worrying about her."

I paused trying to think of the kindest way to break the news to the nurse. Then I said, "Would you like to speak to her mother?"

There was a very pregnant pause. Then she said, "She will be right home."

Review of What We've Done

In this chapter we've further explored the concept of writing about our pasts through the use of vignettes. In particular, we wrote about memorable people in our lives. Now that you have written a couple of sketches about important persons from your past, you should feel confident enough to write a great many more about other people or perhaps more about a specific person.

We also continued to follow the basic format that I introduced in Chapter Three: Brainstorm about possible topics, generate lists, select a particular topic from the lists, explore the topic through the use of the Reporter's 5Ws & H, try a first draft, and work with and play around with the first draft. I'll point out once again that all of these steps are simply *one* format to follow. Sometimes you already have an idea in your head and you're ready to begin writing immediately. That's fine; that's what I do sometimes. The key thing about following some sort of process is that it encourages us to think and re-think about our writing. And the more we think about topics and our writing the more we discover we have to write about.

Let's move on now to Chapter Five and a different kind of writing: Poetry.

Form Poetry

Introduction

You Reading This, Be Ready

Starting here, what do you want to remember?
How sunlight creeps along a shining floor?
What scent of old wood hovers, what softened
sound from outside fills the air?

Will you ever bring a better gift for the world
than the breathing respect that you carry
wherever you go right now? Are you waiting
for time to show you some better thoughts?

When you turn around, starting here, lift this
new glimpse that you found; carry into evening
all that you want from this day. This interval you spent
reading or hearing this, keep it for life—
What can anyone give you greater than now,
starting here, right in this room, when you turn around?

The late William Stafford wrote this poem two days before his death at 79 in 1993. It is a beautiful statement of the joy, excitement, mystery, and insight that he found in everyday life. It is an affirmation of life, of how to live life, that I try to carry with me:

What can anyone give you greater than now,
starting here, right in this room, when you turn around?

What can anyone give us greater than right now, the precious moments that we have left in our lives? Stafford saw glimpses of the eternal in each commonplace moment and tried to capture them through poetry. And poetry, perhaps of all the forms of writing, gives us a special power to capture such moments.

You might be thinking right now that you're not interested in poetry, and that's not the reason you were interested in this book. Perhaps you never read poetry or have never written a poem in your life. All of these might be true, but I know that once you try your hand at poetry and see that it's not the mysterious, difficult thing many people are led to believe by their past schooling you will change your mind. In fact, for some of you reading this paragraph poetry will become your primary form of written expression. Like the 83-year-old woman, Dorothy, in one of my writing classes who had never written a poem in her life but began shortly after joining our group, you might also say, "I can't seem to stop writing poems! Wherever I look I see poetry. My only regret is that it took so long for me to discover it."

"Wherever I look I see poetry." Dorothy understands that poetry comes from our everyday experiences, the most commonplace things: the sparrows at your backyard feeder; the basil that you're chopping for pasta sauce; the photograph of your grandmother hanging in the living room; the toddler romping in the park; the image you recall of a particular picnic with an old friend or lover fifty years ago; the sudden insight you have while walking down the street and see leaves floating through the air in autumn. Poetry is everywhere; it only requires us to look, to see with clearer eyes. That's what William Stafford in his poem was telling us to do—look and see the wonder in the world:

> *When you turn around, starting here, lift this*
> *new glimpse that you found; carry into evening*
> *all that you want from this day.*

I have found that many people are afraid of poetry and avoid it because of how it was presented to them during their years in school and college. Teachers, professors, and textbooks stressed the complexity of poetry, its often unintelligible aspects. It was something that required long and hard study. If students did find a poem that they enjoyed and connected immediately to their lives, say, a love poem while sophomores in high school, all too often their joy was undercut by the teacher's over-analysis and/or the "correct meaning" of the poem. Coupled often with forced memorization of uninteresting poems, such over-analysis led to the future avoidance of poetry. For all-too-many people this avoidance became a life-long abandonment.

The doctor-poet William Carlos Williams whom I've referred to several times said somewhere that "If it ain't pleasure, it ain't a poem!" He didn't mean that all poetry is necessarily cheerful. Quite often we read poetry that is serious, tragic, or that makes us weep. What Williams meant was that in order for a written work to be a poem for an individual he or she must make some emotional connection to it. Otherwise it is nothing more than words on paper—school stuff that we quickly forget.

In this chapter we're going to play around with words and create some easy-to-construct poems. I use the word "play" carefully because that's what poetry is about, playing with language. I've often called poetry the "pyrotechnics" of language, that is, it is language used in its most fiery, volatile, and brilliant manner. Poetry is usually short, compressed, and full of images, and often like an explosive device it bursts into flames of meaning once we ignite it. Thus, we're going to be concerned in this chapter with words and images and we're going to think about and choose them carefully.

We're going to play around with some "Form Poetry," and by that I mean poetry that follows a particular format or structure. Although easy to write, such poetry can often be quite powerful. In a later chapter we will try our hands at more elaborate poetry writing. My purpose here is to help you to have fun and to see that poetry doesn't have to be hard. Accordingly, we will write the following form poems: "Cinquain, "Haiku," "List," and "Couplet." We will begin with the notes and lists you've kept—I hope you've kept them!—from Chapters One, Three, and Four. (If you haven't, don't worry. Your grade won't suffer!) Let's turn to the cinquain.

Writing Cinquain Poetry

"Cinquain" comes from the French and means a collection of five. It is a five-line poem that follows a particular format. Here are three cinquains written collaboratively by small groups of people in one of my Senior writing groups.

Spider
Useful black
Hanging frying washing
Used often by women
Fry-pan

* * *

Kid-curlers
Leather cotton
Curling wiring beautifying
Used mostly by females
Ouch

* * *

Writing
Sweat blood
Thinking struggling rewriting
Desert of unborn ideas
Oasis

As you can see, the cinquain follows a particular pattern:

Line One—one word ("Writing")—gives the title or name of the subject

Line Two—two words ("Sweat blood")—describes the subject in line one

Line Three—three words ("Thinking struggling writing")—describes an action of the subject

Line Four—four words ("Desert of unborn ideas")—expresses a feeling of the subject or a feeling you have about it

Line Five—one word ("Oasis")—renames the subject in line one

The two describing words in the second line are usually adjectives, and the three words in the third line are usually "-ing" words. The fourth line might be a four-word sentence, phrase, or simply four related words. The fifth line is a synonym (or a word meaning something similar) of the word in the first line. We typically don't use any punctuation in cinquains, and you may or may not capitalize the first word in each line.

We can write cinquains about anything. They can be funny, for example, the one above about the old fashioned curlers that women used to use; simply descriptive, such as the one above describing the black cast-iron frying pans that people called "spiders"; or they can be about serious topics, such as the one above about the struggles and joys of writing. Cinquains can be quite literal, such as the one below that I wrote about my mother:

Mom
Beautiful feisty
Caring supporting sharing
I love you so
Helen

Or they can be more figurative, such as the one I wrote about cicadas, those noisy insects that surface in the summer in parts of the Midwest:

Cicada
Ugly noisy
Thrumming sawing praying
Sad frightened regretful lonely
Singer

As you can see, the vital thing about cinquains is the words we use. This is a good place to get out your old thesaurus or purchase an inexpensive one. Words, and our play with them, are the touchstones of cinquains.

Let's Write Some Cinquains

I'm going to use the lists that I made in Chapter One when I was brainstorming about my father's watch. In that chapter we wrote prose pieces about memorable or significant objects in our lives. Objects make for good cinquain poetry. Here are all of my lists from that chapter.

My Object
My father's watch
Gruen Veri-Thin Precision
Silver case
Black minute and hour hands
Red second hand
Military time:
1 to 12 in silver outer ring
13 to 24 in black inner ring
60 second marks in black in most outer ring
Rust spots on face
Cracked crystal
Wind-up watch
"Helen to Frank 46026339" engraved on back
Ticking is loud
Edges of case nicked, scarred, and rough when I rub them
Tastes metallic like a fork
Smells like metal that's been wet and rusted in the past

Who

My father
Construction worker
Died in 1977 at age 61
Born and lived in Chicago
A young hobo during the Great Depression
Work-callused hands
Strong, knobby wrists

When

My mother gave it to him when he left for WWII: "Helen to Frank"

Where

My mother gave it to him in Chicago
My father wore it for over 30 years
I've worn it around the USA & the world since

How

I got it when my father died
It was on his chest of drawers

Why

It's important to me because it reminds me of my father
It's a connection between my father and mother
It's a connection between them and me
It's a symbol of my father's strength
It represents a way of life rapidly fading

Take out all of your lists from Chapter One. If you didn't keep them, then you can brainstorm new lists as we go along. As we've done in the previous chapters, I'd like you to follow me on a separate piece of paper as I write my cinquain. Let's write one first that is quite literal and simply describes our significant objects.

My Cinquain
First line: one word
Gruen

I'm simply looking over my list and have decided to begin with the name of the watch. Select your first word, remembering that the first line is what the cinquain is about.

Second line: two words describing the first line
Military wind-up

I've selected two words to describe the watch in a literal manner. I have several other possibilities, but these are the ones I've chosen for *this* cinquain. Look at your lists and select two words that you like. If you're not sure, use your dictionary or thesaurus.

Third line: three "-ing" words expressing an action
Ticking rusting connecting

The first two words I've chosen actually describe what I see when I look and listen to the watch, but I've chosen "connecting" because I'm going to use it as a link to my fourth line.

Fourth line: four words expressing a feeling of the subject in line one or a feeling you have about it.
My father and me

I'm merely stating that in an important way the watch is a link between me and my dead father.

Fifth line: one word renaming the first line
Frank

My father and I both have the same first name, Frank. Thus, my completed cinquain looks like this:

Gruen
Military wind-up
Ticking rusting connecting
My father and me
Frank

Even though we are writing "literal" cinquains here, I am making a figurative leap, that is, linking "Gruen" with "Frank," and by that I mean both Franks, father and son. That's the nature of poetry, the wonderful thing about it. Once we start writing poems, we naturally find ourselves comparing things in new and unusual ways, using metaphors and similes. (A metaphor says something *is* something else, for example, "A Gruen wristwatch is Frank." A simile says something is *like* something else, for example, "A Gruen wristwatch is like Frank.") Poetry, even such "simple" poetry as cinquains, helps us see the world differently.

Now let's write another cinquain about the same object, except this time we'll try to be less literal and even more figurative. Again, follow along with me on your sheet of paper and be sure to use your lists.

My Cinquain
First line: one word
Hands

As I'm thinking about this poem and looking at my lists, I notice that "hands" are important, both those of a watch and those of my father. Thus, I'm going to build this cinquain around that metaphoric connection. See if you can make a similar connection between two aspects of your object, that is, can you use a metaphor which says one thing is another? Try it.

Second line: two words describing the first line
Scarred steady

In describing the hands of the watch and my father I'm trying to use words that reflect both. Notice that "steady" was not on my lists. As we write and think about appropriate words to use in poems, other ideas come to mind. I also like these two words because of their sound together; they both begin with "s" and have a "ssss" sound. Think about your two adjectives or describing words. Can you also perhaps select two that sound good together?

Third line: three "-ing" words expressing an action
Working weathering remaining

I'm still trying to use words that make a connection through metaphor, between my father's hands and those of the watch. Both hands "work" and have "weathered" time and struggles. The hands of the watch literally "remain," and I'm thinking of how my father's hands 'remain" for me symbolically in the watch. Once again, I also like the way these three words sound together.

I have used two words, "weathering" and "remaining" that were not on my lists. What I'd like you to try here is to use at least one but perhaps two words that were not on your lists. Use your dictionary or thesaurus. Take your time and think about words that will capture the figurative connections between and among aspects of your object. Also consider possible sound play. Don't rush! Words, the right words, are important. I think it was Mark Twain who said that the difference between the right word and just any word to describe something is the difference between lightning and a lightning bug.

Fourth line: four words expressing a feeling of the subject in line one or a feeling you have about it
Around wrist and heart

Here I'm expressing what I feel about my father as his memory continues to live in me through his watch on my wrist. Now I've made an even greater leap through metaphor. I'm saying that my father's hands are not only around my wrist but also around my heart. The watch is a symbol of love. Try your fourth line now. Quite often this is the most difficult line to write in a cinquain. Try a couple of alternatives. For example, at first I thought of using "Wrapped around my wrist," but decided not to use it. Why? Because it really doesn't express a *feeling* about the object; rather, it simply *describes*. I hope you see the difference between these two lines. Give it a go!

Fifth line: one word renaming the first line
Gruen

I'm simply using the name of the watch to capture the concrete object which symbolizes my father. Thus, here's my completed cinquain:

My Father's Watch
Hands
Scarred steady
Working weathering remaining
Around wrist and heart
Gruen

Since it is always possible to tinker with a poem, even a short cinquain, I could rearrange words in the fourth line to read "Around heart and wrist." There's a difference in the two lines: one highlights "wrist" since it comes first in the line, and the other highlights "heart." I like both, and thus I can have two different cinquains simply by changing one line. Look at your cinquain and see if you can play around with one or more lines to give yourself two slightly different poems.

Let's Write Some More Cinquains

Okay, you've probably got the hang of cinquain writing now. The best way to become more comfortable and confident composing them, as with any type of writing, is to try your hand at writing them on a regular basis. You'll see that they are easy and fun to write. I remember one man in a writing class who started writing cinquains and couldn't stop! He laughed and said he had found his "addiction." That's not a bad one to have.

Why don't you go back to Chapter Three and look at the lists that you generated about stories of your life. Select one or more stories, and then from those select important objects about which you might write cinquains. Try this with at least a couple objects. Here's an example of one I wrote about the ghost in my mother's story:

Lorraine
Beautiful hitchhiker
Dancing disappearing yearning
For a warm embrace
Ghost

Spend some time with cinquains, at least a day or two. They will give you confidence in writing poetry and will make it easier as we move on to the second type of form poetry, and that is "Haiku."

Writing Haiku Poetry

Haiku poetry originated in Japan, and some of the most famous haiku poets are Japanese masters. However, haiku are written by people around the world. If you go to any large bookstore and browse in the poetry section, you certainly will find at least one collection of haiku. ("Haiku," by the way is used for both the singular and plural.) Haiku are typically very short two-to-four line poems that express a moment of insight, a flash of recognition, or a sudden inspiration that you might have as you step out onto your back deck in the early morning or as you walk along the lakeshore or in the park. Traditional Japanese haiku almost always dealt with some aspect of nature and with particular seasons of the year. Let's look at some.

Here are two by Basho, perhaps the most famous of all the Japanese masters:

the leeks
newly washed white—
how cold it is

* * *

old pond—
a frog leaps in
water's sound

Here are two more: the first by Buson and the second by Issa:

A flash of lightning!
The sound of dew
Dripping down the bamboos.

* * *

Grasshopper,
Do not trample of pieces
The pearls of bright dew.

Do you see how all four of these are sharp images that capture sudden experiences? The first one, for example, might occur when you're at the sink cleaning leeks for soup. Suddenly their whiteness stabs at you, and you see and feel winter—even though it might be in the middle of summer.

The last one might happen on an early morning walk when all of the insects are damp, cold, and passive and waiting to be warmed by the sun. You glance, and there is a motionless grasshopper on a branch next to a leaf glittering with tiny drops of dew.

There is a mistaken notion that haiku must be arranged according to a particular syllable and line pattern. School teachers often tell their students that haiku must be three line poems of seventeen syllables with five syllables in the first line, seven syllables in the second line, and five in the third. You can see from the four above examples that they don't follow this strict pattern. The mistaken notion has arisen because in Japanese haiku are based upon a particular pattern of *sound*, not syllables. Erroneously, some people have tried to transfer that sound pattern into an English syllable pattern. There's nothing inherently wrong with trying to write haiku this way, that is, in a 5-7-5 syllable pattern. However, I think if you do you will find that you limit yourself. You'll be concentrating on getting the correct number of syllables and not the most vivid words and images.

Let's look at a few more haiku before we write our own. The first one is by a ninety-two-year-old woman; the second by a member of a current Senior writing group, Ardis Kiernan; and the third one by me:

Parsley in the garden
Icy ringlets
Spring

* * *

Sunday afternoon
Cold rain slanting downward
The loon cries

　　＊ ＊ ＊

the odor of lilacs
in a June morning drizzle
mosquitoes hum the chorus

Let's Write Some Haiku

Let's go back to the general list of possible story topics that we brainstormed in Chapter Three. Take out your list. Here's mine:

Stories of "firsts," for example: first day in school, first date, first heartbreak, first job, and so on;
Stories of work: best job and worst job
Stories and family expressions told by parents, grandparents, and other family members;
Stories of childhood or teenage adventures;
Stories about scary experiences, for example, a brush with death;
Stories about "forks" in your life's road;
Stories about "where you were," for example: when World War II ended, when the astronauts landed on the moon, when the millennium began on January 1, 2000, and so forth;
Stories about special places;
Stories about memorable people;
Stories about doing something or making something, for example: canoeing in the Minnesota Boundary Waters Canoe Area Wilderness, walking across the Golden Gate Bridge, giving birth to a set of twins, rebuilding the engine on a first car, and so on;

Stories about how something came to be, for example: how your relatives first came to America, how you got your name, and so forth;

Stories about funny, witty, strange, or sad conversations you overheard or in which you participated.

I'm going to select the Minnesota Boundary Waters Canoe Area Wilderness—a place I love—as the subject about which I'm going to write my haiku. I'd like you to select a favorite nature setting for your first haiku. Ideally, we would all be outside in some natural setting right now, and we'd be looking, touching, listening, smelling, and tasting the richness of the forest, park, garden, riverside, or backyard. We're not, so let's try to work from our imaginations as we re-create our particular favorite spots.

My Haiku Location
Boundary Waters Canoe Area (BWCA)

I'm going to close my eyes and take myself back to all of the times I've been in the BWCA. I'm going to capture all of the things that were special to me when I was there: all that I heard, saw, smelled, touched, and tasted. I'm going to sit quietly as I do this. One of the things that many people like about haiku is that it focuses their concentration. Some people say that haiku is often a kind of meditation, and I agree. Close your eyes and take yourself back to that special place of yours. Sit quietly and focus on that place for at least five minutes.

Okay, now I'm simply going to list the words and images that came to me as I say quietly with my eyes closed. You do the same.

BWCA Words & Images

Beaver lodge
Chewed white beaver sticks
Walleye
Herons
Winding creek
Crescent Lake
Moose
Fisherman's bobber floating
Wind singing in the pines
Frogs singing in the dark
Small birds scratching in the leaves
My father & I when I was a child
My mother on our vacations in Wisconsin
A blood-red sunset
The taste of fir needles on my tongue

Notice that as I sat quietly and re-created my experiences in the BWCA, other related images came to my mind, for example, northern Wisconsin where my family spent its vacations when I was a child. I saw my mother and father there and myself with them as a child.

Now I'm going to take some of these words and images and put them together in some first-draft haiku formats. You do the same, working along with me as I construct my haiku. Let's focus our attempts on those aspects of haiku that I mentioned above: sharp images and flashes of insight or inspiration.

My First Line

Sun shining on Crescent Lake

I want to begin with a visual image: the sun shining on the lake. Now with that image I can picture myself sitting at the lake's edge staring out into the water and listening to the wind in the trees. So my second line focuses on listening.

My Second Line
Wind's melody through the trees

How are your two lines? Do they capture an image? Are you using one or more of the five senses?

As I'm recreating the image of myself sitting at the lake's edge listening to the wind, I suddenly see my mother and hear her humming a song in the little primitive cabin on the banks of the Wisconsin River. Thus, the first two lines serve as a catalyst for a sudden leap for me. Here's my third line.

My Third Line
Mom's lullaby in my ear

Do you have a flash of insight, recognition, or inspiration in your haiku? Is there any word, line, or image that you might change to capture such an expression? Let's look now at the first drafts of our haiku.

My First Draft
Sun shining on Crescent Lake
Wind's melody through the trees
Mom's lullaby in my ear

Is there anything that you could change in your haiku to make if more vivid? As I look at mine I see that the second and third lines deal with hearing, with *sound,* while the first line deals with sight. Thus, I think if I change the first line into one that deals with sound the whole haiku will be stronger. Here's my second draft.

My Second Draft
Sun singing on Crescent Lake
Wind's melody through the trees
Mom's lullaby in my ear

I like my second draft better than the first. Just for practice, I'd like you to change at least *one* thing in your haiku if you haven't done so yet.

We'll do one more together, and then I'll encourage you to write some more on your own. This time let's write one with only two lines, and let's focus on a visual image that suddenly causes us to see things quite uniquely. I'll go back to my list above. You look at yours.

My First Line
The fisherman's bobber

I've started with a simple image, that is, a red-and-white bobber floating gently on the ripples that stir the lake. Is your first line a visual image? Can you *see* the thing?

As I close my eyes and see that bobber floating on the lake I want to capture the spirit of haiku by suddenly shifting the relationship between the bobber and the water. Typically, of course, we would say that the water moves the bobber. But what if we see the relationship differently? What if we reversed things? Here's my completed haiku with its second line.

My Two Line Haiku

The fisherman's bobber
Rocks the whole lake

I like this image; in fact, I think it's more in keeping with the spirit of haiku than my first one since it helps me see the world in a new way. And as I've already mentioned, that's what poetry helps us do: see things freshly. How do you like your second attempt? Better than the first? Might you change anything? Don't worry if you can't get either one of the haiku to "work" for you. You can write *many* more. Everything we write is not going to be marvelous, but some of it will be. The more we write, the better the chance that those extraordinary pieces will emerge.

Try now to write at least two more haiku related to your special place. Use your lists, generate new words and lists, close your eyes again if you need to, and focus on the particular nature of haiku. Here are three more that I wrote about the BWCA.

All sundown the frogs gossiped
The walleye and heron
Eavesdropped on their stories

* * *

Faint scratching in dry leaves
Only a winter wren
Rearranging the world

* * *

The beaver lodge
Littered with white branches
The bones of my father
Will not stay buried

Let's Write Some More Haiku

Although haiku are typically about things in nature and those flashes of insight that we often have, it's also fun just to play around with the form and use it for other, "non-typical" haiku poems. Poetry can be about *anything,* and haiku can be about anything if we want it to be. We don't have to restrict ourselves to what is supposedly "correct" or "proper." Use your general list from Chapter Three again or use any of your other lists and play around with haiku. Try writing them about the most commonplace things. I think once you get into the habit of seeing the world through the lens of haiku, you will be constantly jotting down short poems of all sort. Here are some "non-typical" haiku written by Seniors that might give you ideas. The first two are by Sarah Varner. Notice her humor.

Boyfriend paints his car
Left over green paint
Gravel road makes it stucco

* * *

Frogs jumping across the road
Where are they going
I know where I am:
Fishing

This one by an eighty-eight-year-old woman takes the perspective of the worms being hunted by birds.

Robins chirp worms shudder
Pull into your hole
Quiet—He's gone!

And these two by Dan Kiernan deal with serious subjects.

Old man bent with age
Linking his feeble wife
The Golden Age

* * *

Black child in carnival line
Pushed back by several whites
Love one another

Now give it a go! Why not spend the next couple of days writing haiku when you have an opportunity? As I keep repeating, the more often you write, the more natural it will become.

Writing List Poems

Here's a list poem I wrote about the infant daughter of my niece. We were all delighted with her wonderful wispy hair.

Ode To Madeline's Hair
Tuft of light,
Luminescent halo
Brightening

The dark corners;
Fairy's breath
Soft on thistle seed
Grown young again
Ready to fly;
Wispy top of angel hair
Rising heavenward
In violin notes
Played pizzicato;
Gossamery song
Of laughter
Accompanying
The cricket's reel;
Moonbeams
Dancing on the river,
Stepping to
The salmon's splash;
Strands of wool
Left white on red roses
As the lamb leapt
Over the thorns;
Fingers of God
Reaching out
Into immensity
With caresses of love.

Notice what I've done: I've simply made a list of things that her hair reminded me of, and in this particular poem I've used a lot of metaphors, for example, "Fairy's breath/Soft on thistle seed/Grown young again/ready to fly." But more, I've also paid special attention to the way the word and lines *sound* together, for example, "Played pizzicato," "Stepping to the salmon's splash," and "as the lamb leapt." And I've grouped ideas or images together: the violin notes connected to the cricket's reel, and the cricket's reel leading to the moonbeams dancing to the music of the salmon's splash.

List poems simply describe something by compiling a long or short list related to that person or thing. Each line can begin with any letter or word, and the lines do not have to be of any particular length. Special attention is given to the way words are grouped by sound, idea, and image. List poems can be about any subject, and they can be figurative as the one above, or they can be quite literal. Here's a very simple, literal, one:

> *Desserts*
> *Cakes with cream*
> *Puffed pastries*
> *Strawberry raspberry blueberry*
> *Waffles with whipped cream*
> *Ice cream with whipped cream*
> *Chocolate cherry vanilla*
> *Apple pie with cheese*
> *Cheesecake*
> *Mocha and mousse*
> *Gimme gimme gimme!*

Obviously, this is not a great work or art, and there's no deep meaning to it, but it was fun for me to write. List poems are fun to do. They can be much more serious, of course, and they also give us practice playing around with words, sounds, and images. Notice how I played with sound ("Cakes with cream"; "Puffed pastries"; "Mocha and mousse"), used repetition ("—berry"), and grouped items by type "Chocolate cherry vanilla"). Let's write a couple together.

Let's Write Some List Poems

I'm going back to the lists I made about my father's watch in Chapter One. Take out yours as well.

My Object
My father's watch
Gruen Veri-Thin Precision
Silver case
Black minute and hour hands
Red second hand
Military time:
1 to 12 in silver outer ring
13 to 24 in black inner ring
60 second marks in black in most outer ring
Rust spots on face
Cracked crystal
Wind-up watch
"Helen to Frank 46026339" engraved on back
Ticking is loud
Edges of case nicked, scarred, and rough when I rub them
Tastes metallic like a fork
Smells like metal that's been wet and rusted in the past

Who
My father
Construction worker
Died in 1977 at age 61
Born and lived in Chicago

A young hobo during the
Great Depression
Work-callused hands
Strong, knobby wrists

When
My mother gave it to him when he left for WWII: "Helen to
Frank"

Where
My mother gave it to him in Chicago
My father wore it for over 30 years
I've worn it around the USA & the world since

How
I got it when my father died
It was on his chest of drawers

Why
It's important to me because it reminds me of my father
It's a connection between my father and mother
It's a connection between them and me
It's a symbol of my father's strength
It represents a way of life rapidly fading

I've already got my list. Now in order to write a list poem I have to select what I want to say and how best to say it. This requires me to look closely at the words I choose, the images, and how I group the words and images together. Let's try a simple literal list poem. Follow along with me.

Let's begin with two or more lines that simply describe our things, but let's pay special attention to the way the words sound together. Use what you have in your lists and use other words that come to mind. Here's the start of mine:

My List Poem
Dad's watch
Wind-up and worn
Cracked crystal
Black hands
Hour and minute
Military time

How's yours coming? Notice what I've done is simply to group together aspects of the watch while paying special attention to the sound. Say the start of my list poem out loud and you'll hear what I mean. Do the same with yours. Now let's try a couple of lines that make use of repetition.

My List Poem
Dad's watch
Wind-up and worn
Cracked crystal
Black hands
Hour and minute
Military time
On Dad's knobby wrist
Time
On my narrow wrist
Time

I've repeated "wrist" while contrasting my Dad's wrist to mine and have also repeated "Time." Look at your lines. Play around until you can get at least one repetition. And now let's end our list poems with lines that focus on concluding and important ideas, but, again, let's also be concerned about the way the words and lines sound together. Here's mine:

My List Poem
Dad's watch
Wind-up and worn
Cracked crystal
Black hands
Hour and minute
Military time
On Dad's knobby wrist
Time
On my narrow wrist
Time
"Helen to Frank"
Wife to husband
Husband to son
My father's watch

I've chosen to end my list poem by citing the genealogy of the watch, and by doing so capturing the repetition of "husband," and sounds of "Frank"/"father," "Helen"/"husband," and "Wife"/"watch."

As you readily see, list poems are relatively easy to write, but, like all poetry, they often can take time to write, to say just what you want to say, to use just the words you want to use, and to capture just the images you want to capture. As I have stressed many times, don't try to rush your writing. Take time to mull things over. Play around with words. After you think you have something you like, see if you can say it differently with other words and images. It's in the playing around and experimenting that we often come up with our best pieces of writing.

Let's Write Some More List Poems

I'll leave you to try writing a number of list poems. You might want to return to the lists you made in Chapter Three. Your lists (and any of mine if you choose to use them) should be a rich vein you can mine. Here's a brief list poem based on one of the items I brainstormed in Chapter Three: "Stories of work: best job and worst job." Here's my worst job:

Wendagel's
Steel fabrication
Steel steal
My sixteenth summer
Steel shavings
Rust and red-lead paint
In my hair
In my lungs
In my youth
Scraping rust and steel
Shavings in the summer
Of my sixteenth year

Writing Rhymed Couplet Poetry

Up to now in this chapter on form poetry, we have not discussed rhyme in any detail. We've paid attention to the way words sound together in their beginnings, for example, "Puffed pastries," and at their endings, for example,

"Strawberry raspberry blueberry," but we haven't really looked at the way words might rhyme. That's what we'll do here.

Although we've seen that poetry certainly doesn't have to rhyme, and much contemporary poetry doesn't, I have found in my work with Seniors that many people do like to use rhyme. Perhaps it has something to do with the rhyming poetry of, say, Longfellow, that they remember from their days as schoolchildren. One of the problems with using rhyme is that it is easy to find yourself searching for a word that rhymes and not searching for the *best* word that will express what you're trying to say. It's similar to the problem we saw above with trying to write haiku in a 5-7-5 syllable format: we become locked in by the form when we should be searching for the right word or image.

Rhyming, however, does not have to limit us. In fact, it can often even be used quite effectively in a non-rhyming poem to emphasize an image or idea. The more we play around with rhyme (there it is again, that emphasis on "play"!) the more comfortable, and effective, we'll become with our use of it. Writing rhymed couplets is a good way to begin. A rhymed couplet is simply two lines that have the same, or almost the same, sound at the end. Here's the first stanza of a poem by Emily Dickinson titled "Wind":

> *It's like the light,—*
> *A fashionless delight*
> *It's like a bee,—*
> *A dateless melody.*

We see that Dickinson is using the "—ight" rhyme in the first couplet and "—ee" rhyme in the second one. Sometimes the rhyming words will have the same spelling and sometimes they won't, as in "bee" and "melody." Here's a poem by a member of one of my writing groups who passed away at eighty-eight. Notice how she uses four pairs of couplets and how the last two lines are connected by what we call an "off-rhyme," that is, the two words "cranny" and "any" are very close in sound but not in the same way that "stew" and "you" are.

Dandelions

Their yellow faces greet us everywhere
Upon the hill, the hollow—and over there.
How can we get rid of these jolly faces?
We try our best, but they come up "aces."

We dig, we spray, we cuss and stew
Yet here they are, nodding at you
From every roadside, nook and cranny.
We just can't say, "There aren't any!"

Let's Write Some Rhymed Couplets

If we take the Reporter's 5Ws & H lists that we generated in Chapter Four, we can experiment with writing a variety of couplets about the memorable person we selected. Here are the lists I compiled for John Peterson's father.

Person
Papa

Who
Shoe salesman
Family man

Tolerant of others
Gentleman

What (was special)
Worked long hours six days a week
Walked home for lunch
Never owned a car
Chewed Right Cut Tobacco
Played the Gulbranson piano
Had a sense of humor

Where (did this vignette occur)
Leader Store
Buffalo, Minnesota
Home up the hill from the store
Evening dinner table

When
Great Depression
Hot summer day
One particular afternoon
Later that particular evening

Why
Father greeted all women
Mother was strait-laced, even jealous
John misunderstood father's remark to cute new employee
Mother fumed

How
Mother was silent
Refused to kiss father

Father was confused
Mother bursts into "That girl! Morning Cheer!"
Father clarifies misunderstanding
Family all laugh

If I look at my list, I see that it's pretty easy to write at least a few couplets. Here are some ready examples:

My Papa was a shoe salesman,
Tolerant of others, a gentleman.

My Papa was a family man,
Worked his life as a shoe salesman.

He chewed Right Cut Tobacco,
And played the Gulbranson piano.

Look over your lists and see where you might have rhyming words that you can use to create couplets about your memorable person. If you don't have the ones you want in your lists, don't be afraid to add others or go to the dictionary or thesaurus. Here's such an example:

He worked long hours at the Leader Store
Hoping our family could have a bit more.

Do you get the idea? As you can see, the more you try different words and use such resources as a thesaurus, the more different rhymes and ideas will come to you. Let's try to write one or two more couplets about our memorable people.

He laughed and joked and was of good cheer,
His love wrapped round us both far and near.

We can write couplets that stand alone as two-line poems, and sometimes we can put some of the couplets together to create a longer poem, such as Anne Wren's "Dandelion." See if you can put together any of the couplets you have written about your memorable person. Do they fit? Do they help develop a fuller picture of the person? If not, don't link them together. Here's what I've done with John's father:

My Papa was a shoe salesman,
Tolerant of others, a gentleman.
He chewed Right Cut Tobacco,
And played the Gulbranson piano.
He worked long hours at the Leader Store
Hoping our family could have a bit more.
He laughed and joked and was of good cheer,
His love wrapped round us both far and near.

Let's Write Some More Rhymed Couplets

As I suggested above with the other form poems, cinquain, haiku, and list, practice will help you become more skillful in writing them. Of course, you'll find that you like to write a particular kind more than others. That's okay and only natural. I think it's important, however, that you do indeed try to write all of the different forms. Quite often people who say they have no interest in, say, rhymed couplets, find themselves fascinated by them once they start writing. I've already mentioned the man in one of my classes for whom cinquain writing became an "addiction." Spend some time, say, the next few days, writing couplets when you have an opportunity.

As a bridge to our next chapter and stories about ourselves, let's write at least two couplets about ourselves. Let's write one about an early school experience and then a second about a school sweetheart. Here are mine:

Mother took me out of Eden's Garden
When she marched me off to kindergarten.

* * *

I'll always remember Dolores Peters.
My first kiss was beside the Baltimore Readers.

Review of What We've Done

In this chapter we've written four different kinds of form poetry: cinquain, haiku, list, and rhymed couplet. We've seen that these short poems are easy to write and can express a variety of ideas and moods. The important thing with form poetry, as with any poetry, is that we open ourselves up to it, that we take risks and leap out into the unknown. That's when we often find we can do our best writing and discover new things about language, the world, and ourselves. That's the value and wonder of poetry. It offers us new insights, new images, new worlds. The imaginative psychologist James Hillman says that old age should be a time for turning our lives, experiences, and memories into poetry. He's right.

CHAPTER SIX

Writing Our Lives

Introduction

James Hillman, the imaginative psychologist and author, says in his book *The Force of Character and the Lasting Life* that growing old should be a form of art. It is an opportunity for us to write about and, indeed, to rewrite our lives. Most Seniors now have the time to remember, reflect, reconsider, and reconstruct their past lives. Time is one of the benefits of old age. You now have the time to think about your life, perhaps some of those most important moments or incidents in your life, and to re-invent and re-imagine them. Some Seniors often use this sort of "life review" as an opportunity to come to terms with a difficult time, action, or omission from their pasts. Writing, whether in prose or poetry, helps us in part to make growing old an art form. By re-imagining our lives through writing, we create small works of art that affirm our existence and allow others to share in our joys, sorrows, wonders, and experiences.

In Chapter One we wrote about objects, Chapter Three about family stories, Chapter Four about memorable people, and in Chapter Five we wrote a variety of form poems. Now in this chapter we're going to write about ourselves, our own unique lives. We'll do this by going back to Chapter Three and using the lists we generated there as a starting point. We'll generate some more ideas, and then we'll try our hands at writing both a vignette and a poem about our own particular pasts.

Looking Again at Our Vignette Lists

Let's go back to the lists from Chapter Three of possible things about which we might write vignettes. Find your lists. Here's mine:

Stories of "firsts," for example: first day in school, first date, first heartbreak, first job, and so on;

Stories of work: best job and worst job;

Stories and family expressions told by parents, grandparents, and other family members;

Stories of childhood or teenage adventures;

Stories about scary experiences, for example, a brush with death;

Stories about "forks" in your life's road;

Stories about "where you were," for example: when World War II ended, when the astronauts landed on the moon, when the millennium began on January 1, 2000, and so forth;

Stories about special places;

Stories about memorable people;

Stories about doing something or making something, for example: canoeing in the Minnesota Boundary Waters Canoe Area Wilderness, walking across the Golden Gate Bridge, giving birth to a set of twins, rebuilding the engine on a first car, and so on;

Stories about how something came to be, for example: how your relatives first came to America, how you got your name, and so forth;

Stories about funny, witty, strange, or sad conversations you overheard or in which you participated.

In my work with Seniors, I have found that as they remember and re-imagine their lives in writing they often return to their early years as children and teenagers. That's only natural because these were formative years in which we experienced many firsts, came to understand ourselves and the world, and in a variety of ways shaped our future characters. So, as a topic on which to focus in this chapter, I'm going to select "Stories of childhood or teenage adventures" from my above list. You may follow along with me on this topic or you may choose a different topic from your list. Either way, we'll follow our usual pattern of working together through a piece of writing.

In previous chapters we've been brainstorming lists and using the Reporter's 5Ws & H as techniques to organize our thoughts. I'd like us to try another way of doing so, one that some people find quite useful. It's called "visual mapping." I'd like you to take a fresh sheet of paper, write your topic on top, and follow along with me. Here's the start of mine.

Stories of Teenage Adventures

Draw a circle in the middle of your page and write your general topic in it as I have done in mine:

Now I'm going to think of some *general* kinds of stories about my teenage experiences that I believe are important and say something about my youth and development during those critical years. Then I'm going to represent them visually by expanding my map. Look at what I've done:

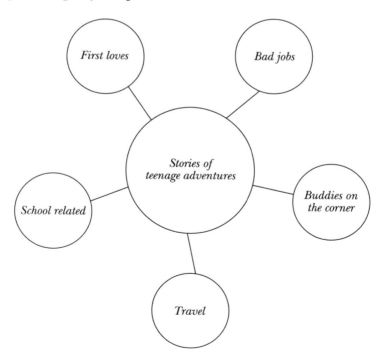

Notice how I've taken the very general "Stories of Teenage Adventures" and have begun to elaborate by drawing out more specific kinds of stories: "First Loves," "Travels," and so forth. These still are rather general, but they begin to get me thinking about particular kinds of stories I might write about. I could probably add more circles than these five, but I think these are enough to give you the idea of how to begin your own visual map.

Now on your sheet of paper do the same thing that I have done above. Start with your main topic circle in the center and add at least four circles that begin to focus on more particular aspects of the topic. Take your time; there's no rush.

Fine. I hope as you are constructing your own visual map you see how this kind of tool for organizing our ideas is different than the simple listing that we've done before. The visual map allows us to *see* possible connections and relationships between and among ideas. Is this kind of organizer better than listing? Not necessarily. Some people like it and regularly use it. I think it can be used effectively *with* listing and the Reporter's 5Ws & H. The more tools you have at hand the better. However, as you write more and more often, you will find what works best for you. There is no one "best" way.

I'm now going to take my visual map above and concentrate on one of the more specific circles, "Buddies on the Corner." Here's what I've done:

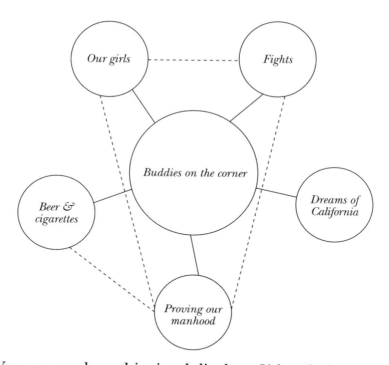

You can see how this visual display of ideas helps me make connections between and among the circles. As I think about adventures, stories, and vignettes of "Buddies on the Corner," certain things come to my mind: "Our Girls," "Fights," "Beer & Cigarettes," "Proving Our Manhood," and "Dreams of California." All of these things were important to us growing up in a blue-collar, working-class neighborhood of Chicago in the 1950s. I have stories to tell about all of these topics and more. Notice, however, in my visual map I can also make the connections between and among these topics. So, for example, getting into fights, drinking beer and smoking cigarettes, and chasing after girls were some of the ways we tried to prove our manhood. I've drawn interrupted lines from these three to "Proving Our Manhood." However, I also see how we often got into fights in order to impress our girlfriends; I've drawn an interrupted line from

"Fights" to "Our Girls" to show that relationship. Once again, visual maps help us see connections that we sometimes miss with simple listing and the Reporter's 5Ws & H.

Now you do the same with your visual map. Focus on one aspect of your original, elaborate on it as I have done, and then draw both uninterrupted and interrupted lines to show the relationships.

Okay, you've got a more elaborate map. Once again I'm going to look even closer at one part of my visual map, and I'm going to think about some very specific stories that I can turn into vignettes of my teenage years.

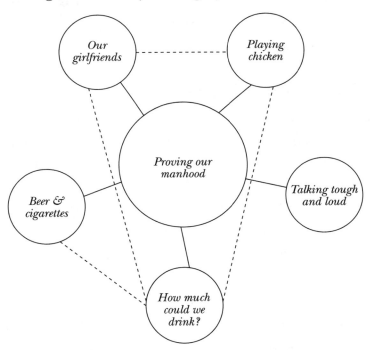

Here's what I've done on my visual map. I've taken the more particular topic, "Proving Our Manhood," and have further expanded it. I've kept "Our Girlfriends" and "Beer and Cigarettes," but I've added two other ways that we as teenagers tried to act like grown men, and that is by "Talking Tough and

Loud," and by "Playing Chicken." Notice that I've also made connections with interrupted lines between "Our Girlfriends" and "Playing Chicken" and "Beer and Cigarettes" and "Playing Chicken." I've done so because as I think about this topic I've decided to write a vignette about how we used to play chicken with cigarettes, and we usually would do so when we drank too much beer and wanted to impress our girlfriends.

What I'd like you to do now is to make some final additions to your visual map. Focus on one specific part of your map that you want to write about and make connections between that particular topic and other things by drawing interrupted lines as I have done.

Let's Write a Personal Vignette

We have our ideas laid out in front of us in our visual maps. Now we're going to use what we've already explored in earlier chapters and begin our personal vignette. Mine is about the general topic of "Teenage Adventures" and one such adventure in particular: how in order to prove our manhood we would play chicken with a lit cigarette in front of our girlfriends. Whether you've decided to also write about a teenage adventure or some other topic, follow along with me as I write my vignette.

We want to have a strong opening sentence or sentences which will catch the reader's attention. Here's my opening paragraph:

> *On my right forearm is a round scar about the size of a dime. It has faded over the years and is hard to see now. I got the scar as a teenager in Chicago during the late-1950s.*

What I've done in my opening paragraph is to use some of the Reporter's 5Ws & H questions, but have omitted the "Why" and "How." I've done that to make the reader curious about why and how I got the scar.

Try an opening to your personal vignette by using one or a few strong sentences that will grab the reader's attention.

Okay? Read your opening out loud a couple of times. How does it *sound* to you? Remember we discussed the importance of reading your writing out loud. It helps you *hear* and also *see* how your piece is shaping up.

I'm going to continue developing my vignette about playing chicken by focusing on the "Why" question in the second paragraph. Write your second paragraph as you continue to develop your vignette.

> *My buddies and I were "tough guys"—or at least we thought we were—and we constantly tested one another as we hung out with our girlfriends on the street corners of our neighborhood. One way of proving our manhood was to challenge someone else to a game of "chicken" with a cigarette.*

Notice that you as a reader now know why we played chicken: we wanted to prove our manhood. Also notice that I'm using the ideas from my visual map about our girlfriends and drinking beer.

Let's continue working on our personal vignettes and write as many paragraphs as necessary. Remember that a vignette doesn't have to be long. Less is usually more. Develop your piece up to the very last and concluding paragraph. Once again, you're in no hurry. Take as much time as you need. Come back to your vignette on another day if you feel "stuck."

> *The game went like this. Two of us would put our forearms together, and then a third person would light a fresh cigarette and place it between our arms. The first person to jerk away his arm was the "chicken."*

In my third paragraph I've now answered the Reporter's question of "How?" I pretty much like what I have up to this point in my vignette, and now I want to think about a strong and effective closing. Our ending should be as attention-getting as our opening. We want the reader to go away with a vivid image in her or his mind. Here's my ending paragraph. You write yours.

> *Oftentimes a whole cigarette would burn out without either person pulling away. As I said, we were tough guys.*

Looking Again at Our First Drafts

Now that we have a first draft of our personal vignettes, let's work with them to see if we can make them any more effective. (Remembering, of course, that we don't always have to write second or more drafts of a particular piece. It all depends on our *purpose* and *audience*. If we want the piece to be more public than private, that is, perhaps be read by people other than our immediate family and friends or we want it to be a legacy to future readers, then we probably want to make it as good as we can. We want to "re-vision" it, see it again.) Here's my complete first draft.

> *On my right forearm is a round scar about the size of a dime. It has faded over the years and is hard to see now. I got the scar as a teenager in Chicago during the late-1950s.*
>
> *My buddies and I were "tough guys"—or at least we thought we were—and we constantly tested one another as we hung out with our girlfriends on the street corners of our neighborhood. One way of proving our manhood was to challenge someone else to a game of "chicken" with a cigarette.*
>
> *The game went like this. Two of us would put our forearms together, and then a third person would light a fresh cigarette and place it between our arms. The first person to jerk away his arm was the "chicken."*
>
> *Oftentimes a whole cigarette would burn out without either person pulling away. As I said, we were tough guys.*

I pretty much like what I have in this little vignette, but I think I can play around with it and make it stronger. Here's my opening paragraph again:

> *On my right forearm is a round scar about the size of a dime. It has faded over the years and is hard to see now. I got the scar as a teenager in Chicago during the late-1950s.*

I'm going to try and make this paragraph more *vivid* and more *specific:*

> *On my right forearm is a round scar about the size of a dime. I burned it into my skin when I was sixteen and*

*hanging out on the street corners of Chicago. It has faded
during the last forty-odd years and is hard to see now.*

Notice what I've done. I've made the paragraph more vivid
by writing "I burned it into my skin" instead of "I got the scar"
and by adding "hanging out on the street corners of Chicago"
instead of simply "in Chicago." I also have made it more *particular* by writing that I was "sixteen" and not merely a "teenager."
I've also replaced "late-1950s" with "forty-odd years."

I like this second version better, and as I read it out loud
it sounds better. But I also could have been happy with the
first paragraph. That's the thing about writing: We can always
play around with our words, sentences, and paragraphs and
try different versions.

What I'd like you to do with your opening paragraph
now is to play around with it a bit. See if you can make at
least two changes which will help your paragraph become
more *vivid* and more *specific.* Think about how you might
change a word or words or how you might even re-write a
complete sentence. Give it a go!

Now I'm going to look at my second paragraph.

*My buddies and I were "tough guys"—or at least we
thought we were—and we constantly tested one another as we
hung out with our girlfriends on the street corners of our
neighborhood. One way of proving our manhood was to challenge someone else to a game of "chicken" with a cigarette.*

Because of the changes I made in the first paragraph I'm
going to have to alter this one too. But more, as I look again

at my visual map I see that I didn't say anything in this vignette about our drinking beer on the street corner. This is important because we would only play "chicken" when we were drinking. Thus, I'm going to rewrite my second paragraph like this:

> *My buddies and I thought we were "tough guys." Sometimes when we drank too much beer and our girlfriends were around, we'd try to prove our manhood by challenging one another to a game of "chicken" with a cigarette.*

I like this paragraph much better than my original attempt. I've taken out "—or at least we thought we were—" and simply wrote "My buddies and I thought we were tough guys." This *sounds* better to me as I read it out loud, and it is "tighter." Notice how I've also included the element of drinking beer as a key factor in our playing "chicken."

Look at your next paragraph. Are there any changes that you might make? Anything you might leave out? Add? Use different vocabulary? Go back and look at your visual maps. Do they give you any additional ideas to include? Try now to make at least one change in your second paragraph. It doesn't have to be a major change; what we're doing here is practicing how we might work with a second draft of a piece of writing.

Here's my third paragraph:

> *The game went like this. Two of us would put our forearms together, and then a third person would light a fresh cigarette and place it between our arms. The first person to jerk away his arm was the "chicken."*

I'm going to make one small, but vital, change to this paragraph in order to make it more specific, more dramatic, and more in keeping with the changes I made in the first two paragraphs.

> *The game went like this. Two of us would put our fore-arms together, and one of our girlfriends would light a fresh cigarette and place it between our arms. The first person to jerk away his arm was the "chicken."*

Notice how replacing "a third person" with "one of our girlfriends" makes this much stronger and dramatic.

Now go through the rest of your vignette and see what possible changes might make it better. Remember you *don't* have to make changes, but the more we at least think about other possibilities, typically the better our writing becomes. Go to it.

Now let's look at our closings. We want the end of our vignettes to be as solid as our opening. We want to leave an image in the reader's mind. Here's my original two-sentence closing paragraph:

> *Oftentimes a whole cigarette would burn out without either person pulling away. As I said, we were tough guys.*

In keeping with the changes I've already made, I'm going to alter the closing as follows:

> *Oftentimes a whole cigarette would burn out without either person pulling away. Our wide-eyed girlfriends thought we were tough guys.*

I've changed the last sentence in order to highlight the role our girlfriends played in this game of proving to ourselves and to them that we were "real" men; moreover, I've added "wide-eyed" to indicate that our game had its desired effect upon our girlfriends.

Now here's my second version of my personal vignette:

> *On my right forearm is a round scar about the size of a dime. I burned it into my skin when I was sixteen and hanging out on the street corners of Chicago. It has faded during the last forty-odd years and is hard to see now.*
>
> *My buddies and I thought we were "tough guys." Sometimes when we drank too much beer and our girlfriends were around, we'd try to prove our manhood by challenging one another to a game of "chicken" with a cigarette.*
>
> *The game went like this. Two of us would put our forearms together, and one of our girlfriends would light a fresh cigarette and place it between our arms. The first person to jerk away his arm was the "chicken."*
>
> *Oftentimes a whole cigarette would burn out without either person pulling away. Our wide-eyed girlfriends thought we were tough guys.*

I like this version more than my first one. Look at your second version. How do you like it? All changes are not necessarily better. Sometimes we rewrite a piece and then discover that our first effort was better. Only you can ultimately decide what you like. However, as most things in life, alternatives often help us see clearer. That's why it's good to get in the habit of playing around with our writing.

To conclude, make any other changes in your personal vignette, read it out loud to hear how it sounds, and then make any last changes. We'll move on now to seeing if we can take our prose vignettes and transform them into poems.

Let's Write a Personal Vignette Poem

In Chapter Five we tried our hand at various kinds of form poetry: Cinquain, Haiku, List, and Rhymed Couplets. We saw that these poems are easy to write and offer us another way of expressing ourselves. Let's conclude this chapter on writing vignettes about ourselves by using our above prose pieces as springboards to personal vignette poems. These also are easy to write.

Why would we want to take our personal vignettes and transform them into poetry? We might do so for the same reason that we often talk about an important event in our lives. The more we express something in various ways, say, a key event from our pasts, the better we often come to understand it and the more interesting it becomes to us and to others. Moreover, poetry is more condensed than prose and highlights particular images through the use of very specific language. Thus, the richness of poetry often gives us an additional sharp image that can complement or supplement our prose writing.

I'm going to look at my prose vignette again. You look at yours also.

On my right forearm is a round scar about the size of a dime. I burned it into my skin when I was sixteen and hanging out on the street corners of Chicago. It has faded during the last forty-odd years and is hard to see now.

My buddies and I thought we were "tough guys."
Sometimes when we drank too much beer and our girlfriends
were around, we'd try to prove our manhood by challenging
one another to a game of "chicken" with a cigarette.

The game went like this. Two of us would put our fore-
arms together, and one of our girlfriends would light a fresh
cigarette and place it between our arms. The first person to
jerk away his arm was the "chicken."

Oftentimes a whole cigarette would burn out without
either person pulling away. Our wide-eyed girlfriends thought
we were tough guys.

Reading what I have here and then closing my eyes and trying to visualize all of us on those street corners so many years ago, particular images come to my mind's eye. I see all of us so-called "tough guys" in our faded Levis, t-shirts, and leather jackets. I also see how we would hang around, strut, and often preen for our girlfriends thinking we looked like Elvis Presley or James Dean. I'm going to try a few lines that capture that image. You do the same. Close your eyes and try to *see* what your prose piece is about. Remember, you want to capture specific images. Here's my first attempt:

Tough guys in Levis and leather jackets
Loafing under a corner street light
Pitching pennies and posing like Elvis

As I wrote the first two lines I suddenly remembered that we used to pitch pennies to pass the time. I haven't thought of that in years! It was in the writing that that particular memory surfaced. Once again, writing has a way of doing that.

Now that I have the image of us on the street corner I'll try to capture the key elements in my prose vignette, that is, how we drank beer, showed off for our girlfriends, and burned our arms all in the attempt to assert our manhood, or at least what we thought our manhood should be like:

Drinking beer talking of California
Testing ourselves for our girlfriends
With lit cigarettes on our skinny arms

Notice that as I develop my poem I'm trying to do a few things. First, I'm trying to create particular images or pictures through my choice of words, for example, "posing like Elvis" and "our skinny arms." Although I'm not using any sort of rhyme, I am conscious of how the words sound together. Thus, I'm looking at the way the words support one another, for example, the "l" sound in "Levis," "leather," and "loafing," and the "p" sound in "pitching," "pennies," and "posing." Then in the second three lines I'm using "-ing" words to help carry the poem along: "drinking," "talking," and "testing." Lastly, I'm trying to keep all of my lines around the same length. If you count the syllables in each line, you'll see that each line roughly has around ten syllables.

Continue to develop your poem focusing on particulars and vivid images. Then look it over and see what you have up to this point. See if there are any words that you might change or add to make your poem flow or "work" better. What about line length? Read your poem out loud. *Poetry must be heard!*

Now I'm going to try the last lines of my personal vignette poem.

Wondering how it was to be men
Thinking that seared flesh and gritted teeth
Might somehow magically show us the way.

Here's the first draft of my poem:

Tough guys in Levis and leather jackets
Loafing under a corner street light
Pitching pennies and posing like Elvis
Drinking beer talking of California
Testing ourselves for our girlfriends
With lit cigarettes on our skinny arms
Wondering how it was to be men
Thinking that seared flesh and gritted teeth
Might somehow magically show us the way.

I pretty much like what I have, but I'm not that happy with the last few lines. I'm going to play around with them, revise (or look again), and see if I can make the poem stronger. I don't like the line "Wondering how it was to be men"; it's too obvious; it *tells* when it should *show*. I'm going to get rid of it, and I'm going to change the last two lines. Lastly, I'm going to remove "our" from "our skinny arms"; I don't like the over use of "ourselves," "our girlfriends," and "our skinny arms." Now my poem reads:

Tough guys in Levis and leather jackets
Loafing under a corner street light
Pitching pennies and posing like Elvis
Drinking beer talking of California
Testing ourselves for our girlfriends
With lit cigarettes on skinny arms

Thinking that seared flesh and gritted teeth
Would magically show us the way

I like this better. The last line requires the reader to make the connection concerning "the way" that we were looking for as teenagers. I'm not telling the reader, and he or she might see several possible interpretations. That's the value of poetry: possible meanings.

Now look over your poem again. Play around with it until you're happy with what you have. As I did, you might think about the way words sound together, the length of your lines, the images you're creating in the poem, and how your poem might lend itself to a richness of meanings when read by different readers. I think if you put your poem alongside your prose vignette, you'll see that there is an added value to your particular story. I know there is in mine.

Review of What We've Done

In this chapter we've continued to develop our ability to capture the past by writing vignettes. However, in this particular case we've written about our own pasts in personal vignettes. We've also tried another way of generating ideas and organizing our thoughts, and that is with visual mapping. Such maps are often useful by themselves or when used in conjunction with listing and the Reporter's 5Ws & H. The value of visual maps is that they often help us make connections between ideas that we might sometimes miss. We also looked again at revising our first drafts and saw how valuable such revision can be.

After we completed our prose personal vignettes we used them as springboards to personal vignette poems.

These poems add an additional dimension to our life stories by highlighting specific images and calling attention to the key elements of the particular vignette. We also saw the value of looking again at the first drafts of our poems and paying attention to specific elements that might help make them stronger.

Fathers and Sons

Let's pause now to reflect on what we've done up to this point in the book. We've considered the importance of writing in an effort to remember, explore, and preserve for ourselves and others our unique lives and experiences. We've written about objects that have some meaning or importance to us. We've remembered and written about memorable family stories, people, and our own lives. And we've tried our hands at various kinds of form poetry that help us present our pasts in different ways. Moreover, we've looked at several "tools of the writer's trade," such as how to generate ideas through the Reporter's 5Ws & H, visual mapping, and how to revise or to "see again" a piece in progress.

I hope it is becoming clearer as we write that growing old, as James Hillman maintains, is not simply a biological process. It is also an art form, or at least it can be a form of art. As we write we see that our lives are not somehow permanently etched in granite. The more we think, talk, and write about them, we see that there are possible ways of looking at our lives. Memory, someone once observed, is the realm of the must-have-been. It is not a fixed thing. As humans we are natural storytellers, and the stories we tell and write about our memories help us to shape and re-shape our lives.

We all have suffered—some much more than others—sorrows, fears, losses, and disappointments. We might have lost a spouse after many years of marriage. A child might have died suddenly. Our youthful dreams and ambitions might have come to little. We might regret certain decisions we made and paths we took in our lives. Our health might be failing us and we fear future illness and debilitation. Indeed, if we reflect seriously, I think we all will see that there is a thread of grief that runs through our lives.

It is precisely this thread of grief that gives our lives vitality. Our sorrows, fears, and losses help give our joys and loves their vigor. Quite often the most persistent and memorable stories that we tell and re-tell are those that deal with certain difficult times in our lives, certain failures, and particular sadnesses. Why do we come back to these stories again and again? I think it is because in the telling and re-telling we are trying to transform them into something different, something understandable and meaningful. We are struggling to turn our lives into art.

Thus, I think as we continue to write we should be open to *all* aspects of our lives and not only to those pleasant experiences and warm memories. The more curious we are about those less pleasant or painful experiences and those "darker" memories, the more we will understand them and possibly transform them into something we can readily acknowledge and hold. To cite James Hillman once again, he says that we should not be concerned with "knowing" ourselves in old age; rather, we should be concerned about "discovering" ourselves. The more we write the more we will discover the hidden places in our lives.

Let me end this interlude with a personal example. My father died over twenty years ago, and like most fathers and sons we had a complex relationship. There were times of love and comradeship and others of anger and hostility. For many years after my father died I ignored or repressed a particular incident in which he had failed me. It was painful to both of us, and we never discussed it while he was alive. After his death I especially regretted never talking to him about it. I carried this buried grief around with me for many years until finally I wrote about it. In the poem I forgave my father his failing and connected to him in spirit. The poem helped me transform a hurtful past into a life-affirming present. Art overcame sorrow.

Fathers and Sons

God damn it, the essence of art is life, not death.
—William Carlos Williams

My father, drunk,
Pulls a pocket-knife on younger men
And gets punched in the face:
Forty years later and I still hear
The crack of a fist on his cheek.
And then I a skinny 16-year-old
Kid flailing to his rescue,
Only to be pounded down into a ball
To protect my head from random heels.

During these moments of fury,
While the men forget I am a boy,
My father stands slack-armed and watches.

The unspoken grief we carry inside us
That connects fathers to sons.
We never talked of those 30 seconds
On the oil-and-spittle-covered floor
Of a subsequently demolished gas station.
I hid my speechless sadness inside
Like an unsightly, unhealing sore
Which time helped to conceal, but never cure.
What wounds and tongue-less demons
Tormented my father's heart I only imagine.

The losses that separate fathers and sons,
And the countless inconsequential acts
That unite them across time, across space,
Across the chasm between life and death:

My father and I under my first car,
Supported by jacks and railroad ties;
We on our backs in our own garage
Wrestling with a rotten exhaust system.
My father's knuckles bloody from repeatedly
Cracking them against the unyielding metal;
I rapidly blinking tears from the motes
Of rust and mud lodged in my eyes.
"Hand me that 1/2-inch open-ended wrench,
Son, this sonofabitch won't work!"

Across time, across space, across death,
I find the half-inch and hand it to him

With our shoulders side-by-side on the floor,
And for an instant our hands together on the wrench:
Bloody knuckles and a dirty thumb brush fleetingly.
In that gesture a blessing, a forgiveness,
From father to son, from son to father.

CHAPTER SEVEN

Photographs and Writing

Introduction

We've often heard people say that "a picture tells a thousand words." Well, yes and no. The picture doesn't tell the thousand words; it elicits them. *We* do the telling as we look at and talk about the picture; it can stir our memories and call up stories of our pasts. In this chapter we'll look at how we can use photographs to write about our lives.

Why Photographs?

In my work with Seniors I have found that most people like to reminisce about old photographs. Looking through the albums that hold pictures of our parents when they were young, of ourselves when we were children and young adults, of our own children and grandchildren, and of all the people that we've known in our lives calls up words, images, and stories. I have spent many enjoyable hours sitting around a workshop table while Seniors shared old, often faded, black-and-white photographs. The stories that they told about those photographs were then sometimes written down. Here's one by Dorothea after she shared a photograph of her father.

My Best Friend
by Dorothea Nielsen

My best friend was my daddy. He was kind and loving, but strict. I would ask him so many questions about history, or our government, or geography. He was my teacher out of school.

I can remember him taking us four girls, Edna, Lois, Edith, and myself on his knees and giving us horseback rides. He did this every evening after supper.

I would work with him in the fields picking rocks and fixing fences. At time for regular chores I noticed that when my dad raised his voice all the livestock in the barn moved. They knew who was boss.

When he and Mother got their barn clothes on they would sing "Pretty Red Wing" and dance around the kitchen table.

Once when yo-yos were in, my dad and I spent a whole day making one. It took some doing to get it balanced just right, but we succeeded. Another time we made a boomerang, and that took all day, but we succeeded. It was neat to throw it and have it come back to you.

In the summer evenings Daddy would play ball or sometimes horseshoes. We thought it was so nice that he would play with us. He was one of us.

In the winter he showed us how to hold our sleds to our bodies, run, drop down on a hard icy surface, and slide a long way. Again, he was just like us kids.

I also remember the day my daddy showed me how to start the gasoline engine to pump water for the livestock.

Daddy was great with his patience to teach us how to do things. He'd show me how a thing was done, and then I did it until it was right.

When Daddy took a wagon load of grain to town to have it ground into feed for the stock, we'd see him coming down the road. I would run down to meet him, and he'd stop and pick me up.

My daddy was my best friend, and I loved him.

You see how a single photograph brought forth from Dorothea all of these fond and *particular* memories of her father and her childhood? (Remember that the best writing is about *specific* things!) Let's try our hands at writing about some of our own photographs.

Selecting the Photographs

We can of course write about any photograph, but typically we will select those that evoke some special memory or cause us to ask more questions about them. The memories stirred by photographs are not always the pleasant ones that Dorothea captured in the piece about her father. Sometimes they are disturbing or painful or full of sadness. Likewise, we might find ourselves puzzling over a photograph about which we don't know the whole story. It might lead us into further research into our own pasts. Ultimately, you will decide which photographs and which stories you will want to capture and preserve for future generations.

We'll begin by writing about ourselves, and then we'll try a second piece about a photograph of someone else or of several other people. I'm going to select a photograph of myself as a child growing up in an inner-city ethnic neighborhood of Chicago in the 1940s and 1950s. I'd like you to look through your photographs and find one of yourself as a child. Pick one that takes you back to a particular time and place and that enlivens your senses as you look at it. Here's mine.

The Reporter's 5Ws & H strategy that we've been using is especially good for an initial look at a photograph. Let's try it here. On a separate sheet of paper follow along with me as I list some essentials about my photograph.

My Photograph
Me on a blind horse

Who
Me as a child of about 8 or 9

What
Having my picture taken in my cowboy outfit by the traveling photographer who would come to the neighborhood with his blind horse

Where
2714 Hillock Avenue in Chicago; the neighborhood is called Bridgeport

When
This was around 1951

Why
I pestered my mother to have my picture taken on a "real" horse

How
The photographer used an old-fashioned, large, and cumbersome camera that required me to sit still for more than a minute while he took the picture from beneath a black hood

Do you have your 5Ws & H on your sheet of paper? If not, look closely at your photograph and, using my list as an example, complete yours. Let's continue once you have that done. If the first picture you've chosen isn't "working" for you, try another. You can always return to your first selection.

Okay, now that we have an initial listing of who, what, where, when, why, and how let's look again. I have found that the value in writing about photographs is that once we begin to think, talk, and write about them they arouse so many other images and memories. I simply could write a short sketch of how one summer afternoon I persuaded my mother to let me have my photograph taken on a blind pony. It would be interesting and capture a time and way of life that no longer exists in inner-city Chicago. Photographers don't travel around with blind ponies; ragmen don't come through the alleys with horse and wagon; and icemen don't carry blocks of ice into kitchens on their rubber-padded shoulders anymore. But as I continue to look at and think about this photograph other images and ideas come to my mind. Let's use the Reporter's 5Ws & H to expand our ideas about our photographs. Once again, on your sheet of paper follow along with me.

My Photograph
Me on a blind horse

Who
Me as a child of about eight or nine
My imaginary friend, Jimmy
My imaginary girlfriend, Betty
My cowboy heroes, Hopalong Cassidy and Roy Rogers
Wild stallions

What
Having my picture taken in my cowboy outfit by the traveling photographer who would come to the neighborhood with his blind horse
My imaginary cowboy adventures with Jimmy
The day I lost Jimmy and discovered Betty

Where
2714 Hillock Avenue in Chicago; the neighborhood is called Bridgeport
Grandpa's yard and garden
The neighbor's garage
The alleys, prairie, and steel yard near our house

When
This was around 1951
The Wild West era of cowboy movies

Why
I pestered my mother to have my picture taken on a "real" horse

I lived the imaginary life of my cowboy heroes
I fell in love with the actress Dale Evans
I created a pre-adolescent love affair

How

The photographer used an old-fashioned, large, and cumbersome camera that required me to sit still for more than a minute while he took the picture from beneath a black hood

My rich imagination allowed me to create whole worlds and people in my grandfather's yard

My mother never discouraged my imaginary play

You see what further exploration of my photograph has done for me? It has helped me to recall the imaginary world of my childhood. In particular, it helped me remember *specific* people, both real and imaginary, places, and events that I have not thought of in more than forty years or so. Further exploration of the photograph has stimulated other ideas for a vignette, one different from my original thoughts. Clearly, I can write about having my picture taken on a blind pony in 1951, and that would be fine. However, I'm now excited to write about something else related to my cowboy picture, and that is my imaginary adventures as a Wild West hero and the first love of my young life.

Now your additional exploration of your photograph might have taken you in any number of directions. It might have helped you recall as mine did some related ideas or adventures. It might have helped you probe deeper into your first memories. Or it might have simply given you more vivid images. Regardless of which direction your further thinking about your photograph is leading you, I hope you can see the value of spending some time with each picture you might want to write about. Always try to go beyond your initial thinking and brainstorming.

Let's Try a First Draft

We have ideas and direction from our two above listings. We can now use them to begin the first drafts of our photograph sketches. Let's try an opening paragraph, remembering the importance of a beginning sentence that will grab the reader's attention. Use a new sheet of paper, and I will write mine below.

> *My sidekick Jimmy and I rode through Grandpa's yard on wild Appaloosa stallions. We let them gallop flat out as we pursued the gang of grizzled outlaws who had robbed the bank and murdered one of the tellers. The horses ran with crazy, walleyed abandon, their foam-flecked muzzles and labored breathing signaling impending collapse.*

What I'm trying to do in my opening paragraph is to capture the cowboy movie and comic book imagery that so enthralled me as a child. I'm also trying to be as vivid as possible: horses running with "crazy, walleyed abandon" and ready to collapse with "foam-flecked muzzles." Note how the blind pony on which I sat for the photograph became a "wild Appaloosa" stallion in my imagination.

Look at your opening paragraph. Do you have a strong beginning sentence? Is your writing descriptive and specific? Say it out loud. Can you see, hear, feel, taste, or smell some of the things you're writing about? If not, see if you can make your opening sentence and paragraph more vivid. Once you have done so, let's continue.

> *We finally caught up with the miscreants at the pass between Grandpa's garden and Mrs. Dudek's garage. They decided to make their stand there instead of heading into the mountainous high country where we surely would have lost them.*
>
> *The gunfight was short, but furious and deadly. Jimmy while still riding at breakneck speed, shot two of the men with his Winchester 30-30. His horse then stumbled, trapping him, and I had to face the other three alone. I leapt off my horse and challenged them to draw. They laughed when they saw that I was only a kid with a single pearl-handled 45 strapped to my hip.*
>
> *They didn't laugh long, however. I drew with the blinding speed I had learned from Hopalong Cassidy and fired with the accuracy Roy Rogers had taught me. In an instant the three outlaws lay dead amidst Grandpa's string beans.*

How is your sketch coming along? Notice how I am continuing to develop what I began in the first paragraph. I'm combining the actual world of my childhood surroundings with the transformed world of my imagination; thus, there is a mountain "pass" between "Grandpa's garden and Mrs. Dudek's garage." I'm still incorporating the cowboy movie and comic book language of the time, "miscreants," and trying to be specific in my descriptions: "Winchester 30-30" and "pearl-handled 45."

Check to see if your piece is further developing the ideas and images in your first paragraph. Is the story of your photograph building? Will someone, say, fifty years from now be interested or intrigued by what he or she is reading? Let's go on.

Jimmy and I rode back into town with the sacks of money taken from the bank. There was much cheering and fanfare for us. "Hurrah for the Arizona Kid!" the town storekeepers shouted as I passed. We tied our horses to the hitching-rail in front of the saloon, and I grabbed a fresh cigar from the catalpa tree that grew by Grandpa's back window. I was about to light it when I saw her.

She was standing out of the dust on the wooden sidewalk. Her long black hair cascaded down to her shoulders, and her brown eyes and perfect smile were so dazzling that I stood speechless. She was dressed like Dale Evans and had two silver pistols strapped to her boyish hips. I dropped my cigar and walked over to meet her.

Until I began writing this sketch I had forgotten that I called myself the "Arizona Kid"! It was in the re-creation of my cowboy adventures that it came back to me. The catalpa tree in my grandfather's yard was a source of pleasure for me as I would pretend I was smoking the long, slender pods that came from it. I have not thought of that tree in decades, and it is not in the photograph. Again, we can see the value of writing about the past: all of these little details surface. Of course, you can see the influence of Dale Evans upon my imagination. I'll continue with my sketch; you continue with yours.

My imaginary and best friend Jimmy disappeared that day. He walked into the saloon, and I never saw him again. My mother stopped setting a place for him at the dinner table and was pleased that I no longer carried on long conversations with the air.

The photograph of me on a blind pony has not only led to remembrance of my childhood imaginative adventures, but it also has resulted in an indirect observation about my mother. Notice in the above paragraph that I comment on how my mother was relieved that I stopped talking to my imaginary playmate. However, also notice that she used to set a place at the dinner table for him. The reader thus gets a glimpse into my mother's character.

> *She never knew that Betty had come into my life. Betty of whom I never spoke, but with whom I traveled the Wild West for the next year or so. Together we rode side-by-side, through every corner of Grandpa's yard, over into the neighboring prairie, across the back alley, and even through the steel yard of the fabrication plant next door.*
>
> *Our fondness for each other grew daily, and, I guess, it was something like love. Like most secret loves, however, it was destined to fade. One autumn morning with tears in her eyes and a lump in my throat, Betty rode south and I turned north.*
>
> *I still think of her at times. When fall turns the world brittle and gold and I walk under a catalpa tree, I still pluck a cigar, put it between my teeth, and remember Betty with her brown eyes and matchless smile.*

That's the rest of my first draft about my photograph. I continued to combine the actual world of my childhood, for example, "steel yard of the fabrication plant next door," with my imaginary world, for example, "Betty rode south and I rode north." In my last paragraph I brought the photograph into the present. Now, after writing this vignette, that time and place, that childhood world, once again lives in me.

I can now begin to look again, to "re-vision," my first draft, and you can begin to reflect on yours. Since we already have engaged in the revision process several times in previous chapters, we will not go through it now with our photograph sketches. Look over your first draft, however. Even if you decide not to make any changes or even if the piece that you wrote is one that you don't especially want as a "keeper," it's always good practice to re-read our first efforts. And, once again, read out loud. How does it sound? Is your language vivid? Is there anything that could be added to make it more descriptive and lively? Is there anything that you could leave out? Does your opening grab the reader's attention? Lastly, is your closing such that the reader will remember what he or she has read?

Let's Try a Couple of Other Photographs

Now that we have written about one of our photographs, let's play around with a couple more. With these two we'll just explore and practice how to generate and organize our ideas. We'll only write opening paragraphs to these two vignettes. For the first, let's again select a pictures of ourselves as children, but also one that includes other people. And for the second let's pick a photograph of some memorable persons in our lives.

As you can see from the picture I've selected, I'm going to stick with my cowboy theme. Do you have yours? Is it one that you really like? Don't waste your time writing about something for which you're lukewarm. Okay, now that we each have a photograph, take a clean sheet of paper and let's generate ideas by using the visual mapping technique

we tried in Chapter Six. Follow along with me on your paper as I generate the visual map for my photograph.

*Playing cowboys in
Grandpa's yard*

What I've done in order to begin my visual map of the photograph is to draw a circle and to label the central theme. This photograph is about how we used to play cowboys in the yard. That's me holding the gun. Do the same thing on your sheet of paper. Draw a circle in the center, look again at your photograph, decide on the central theme or idea of the photograph, and in a few words write that theme in the circle.

Now let's look more closely at our photographs and begin to add "arms" to our visual maps. Here's my first arm.

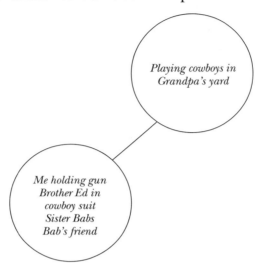

The first arm of my visual map simply deals with the people, or *characters,* in the photograph: myself; my younger brother, Ed; my older sister, Babs; and one of my sister's friends whose name I don't remember. What is the first arm of your map? Does it capture the people in the photograph? Perhaps there are animals in yours? Regardless of what you focus on, the first arm of your visual map should begin to help you organize your ideas.

Now I'm going to expand my visual map by adding two more arms: one dealing with the location, or *setting,* of the photograph; and the second dealing with the what's going on, or the *action,* that's taking place. You might expand yours in a similar manner, if appropriate. If it's not appropriate to expand yours by adding setting and action, then add at least two more arms that capture key elements of your photograph.

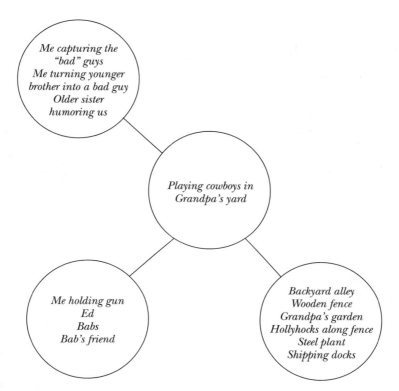

How is your visual map progressing? How does it look? Is it capturing the key elements of the photograph? By looking at the photograph and organizing your ideas are you also able to remember other details? For example, in my photograph you cannot see any hollyhocks along the wooden fence in the background. However, that's one central image that stands out in my memory of that yard: The huge hollyhocks that grew wild each summer and which were a buzzing haven for bees. Thus, I've included that in my circle that deals with the setting.

Is there anything else in your photograph that you'd like to add to your visual map? Any other key elements or images that you know were vital to the world of that photograph but perhaps were outside of it as it was taken? If there's anything else, perhaps add another arm, or even two, to your map.

I'm going to add one more to mine, one dealing with the cowboy suits my brother and I were wearing.

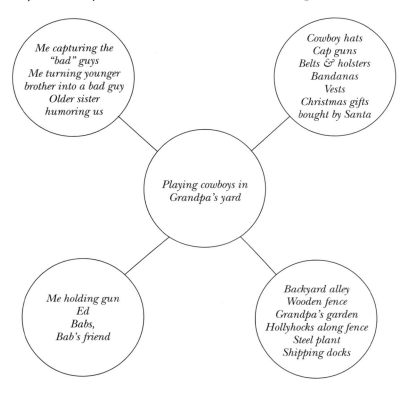

There's my map. The last circle, or arm, that I added deals with the cowboy outfits that my younger brother and I received the previous Christmas. We had pleaded with our parents to convince Santa Claus to bring us complete outfits with guns, holsters, hats, and so forth. And indeed on Christmas morning that's what we found under the tree! How is your visual map? Does it capture most of the vital elements of your photograph? Remember, as I discussed in Chapter Six, visual mapping is *one* way of generating and organizing ideas before we begin to write. Some people like it and use it a lot; others prefer the 5Ws & H. You know what works best for you; however, visual mapping works well for generating ideas about photographs. It's a visual way of dealing with a visual object.

Let's use our maps to begin our vignettes, or stories, about our photographs. We'll only do the first paragraph together. You can continue your vignette later. Let's try to get an interesting and arresting first sentence. Here's mine:

> *Santa Claus wasn't concerned with gun control in the late-1940s.*

I think that opening sentence will cause the reader to want to know what Santa Claus has to do with gun control. The sentence came to me as I looked at my visual map and thought about me holding the cap gun, Santa bringing it to us, and current thinking about firearms and children. The photograph and my visual map helped me connect the past to the present. How's your first sentence? Will it lead the reader into your story? If you're not sure, try another version of it.

Now let's complete our opening paragraphs by focusing on one of the arms of our map, that is, the arm with which you began. I started with the one that dealt with our cowboy outfits, so that's how I'll continue.

> *Santa Claus wasn't concerned with gun control in the late-1940s. He was quite willing to arm and outfit a couple of young buckaroos with cap guns, holsters, vests, bandanas, and jaunty cowboy hats.*

That's my opening paragraph. Notice how I used the elements in the one visual map arm to describe what is contained in the photograph. I also used language appropriate to the picture and the time, that is, "buckaroos," and I tried to find an adjective that captured the hats that we wore, that is, "jaunty."

How's your opening paragraph? Does it take the reader into the photograph and will it lead him or her into your story? Have you thought about the language that you're using? Is it appropriate to the picture? Are there better words that you might use? Now's another appropriate time to take out your thesaurus and browse. Lastly, notice how my opening paragraph contains only two sentences. Our writing doesn't have to be overly long. As I've already mentioned several times, less is more.

Continue writing your vignette about this particular photograph. Once you have something that you like, have re-read it, and perhaps have worked on a revision, come back to this section. We'll move on to another photograph. Don't rush yourself, however. Take all the time you need, even days perhaps, before you return.

A Photograph of a Memorable Person

We wrote about memorable people in Chapter Four. Sometimes a photograph will call to mind such people and specific things about them. When we browse through photographs, quite often we remember particular characteristics of the individuals captured on film, or we laugh as we suddenly remember a story or incident involving the person who is staring back at us from the picture. Photographs of people are wonderful memory aids; that's one of the reasons we take them. As such they can serve as great catalysts for our writing. I know one Senior who wrote hundreds of pages of stories, poems, and sketches about the people in her photograph albums. Let's try the beginning of such a sketch.

Look through your photographs and select one of a person who is or was important in your life or one of a person who brings to mind an interesting story. As my example I'm going to use a photograph of my father when he was a young man and working in a Chicago foundry. Here's the photograph:

Do you have yours? After you have chosen one, keep it on the table or desk in front of you and follow along with me on a new piece of paper.

This photograph of my father who was born in 1916 must have been taken in 1935 or 1936 after he had returned to Chicago from several years of hoboing around the country. It was during the dark years of the Great Depression and a couple of years before he and my mother were married. My father often told stories of working as a molder in several small foundries during those difficult years.

Let's practice looking closely at our photographs. The more we look, the more we usually see. Sometimes we look at photographs but do not really <u>see</u> all that's in them. I'm going to look at the photograph of my father in the foundry and make a list of nouns that I see in it; that is, I'm going to make a list of *persons* and *things*. You do the same with your photograph and on the new sheet of paper.

Persons
Dad—second from left, skinny young man with arms at his side
Man with iron rod and dirty face—farthest left behind my father
Shorter stocky man—to the right of my father
Older man—farthest right, probably the foreman, perhaps Lithuanian immigrant

Things
Mound of black sand that appears to be five- or six-feet high
Two shovels behind my dad, one must be his
Shelves against the brick wall with some cans and containers
Ladder against the back wall—leading to where?
Four windows letting in sunlight, one directly above my dad
Steel girders, cables, chains, pulleys
Brick walls—black from smoke and grime
Large chain and "S" hook in the center
Cogs, huge gears, wheels
Two molds—one in front of Dad and one in foreground
Two paint cans on foreground mold, black brush on top of one
Bottom of a push broom on foreground mold
Huge vat on far right for molten metal
Cable that looks like a noose hanging behind man on far right

That's my list of nouns. I could get even more detailed if I wanted, but I think this list gives me a close enough look at the photograph. How's your list? Is it as long as mine? Longer? Don't be afraid to list the most seemingly insignificant person or things in your photograph. Quite often it's these things that generate the most interesting writing.

Now that we have looked closely at our photographs and made lists of what we see in them, let's use those lists to begin writing. We'll begin three different pieces about our photographs. I want you to see that you have several possibilities when it comes to capturing in words what you see in the picture.

Describing What We See

The first possibility is simply to write a vignette about what we see in the photograph, using what we know about it from first-hand experience or from stories we heard about it. Let's try an opening paragraph in this manner. Use your list of nouns and the photograph itself to begin your vignette. I'll start mine below. Remember to try and grab the reader's attention in your opening.

My dad could shovel black sand twelve to fourteen hours a day, and he often did so with a Camel cigarette hanging from his lips. The small foundries in which he worked during the Great Depression were brutal places of smoke, cogs, wheels, pulleys, and chain-swinging molds that could crush a foot or take a hand. My dad worked in these Chicago foundries for two years because he was skilled at pouring molten metal and because it was the best work he could find.

166 Exploring Our Lives

That's my opening paragraph. I'm using the photograph, my list of nouns, and the stories I remember my dad telling us (shoveling sand for fourteen hours) to create a beginning to my vignette that I hope will intrigue the reader. From this *first draft* beginning I can continue to develop the vignette and then work with it in a second draft if I so choose. How is your opening paragraph? Have you used the photograph itself, your list of nouns, and what you know about the picture? What's your first sentence like? Read it out loud. How does it sound to you? Might you add something to it to make it more interesting and specific? (Notice how I used "a Camel cigarette hanging from his lips" to try and make it so.) Now let's leave these openings to our vignettes and try a second way of capturing photographs in words.

Using First Person Perspective

Sometimes with a photograph we remember the person in it talking about the situation or event which the photograph captures. His or her words come back to our mind. We can use what we remember to write about the photograph from that person's point of view. We can write as if that person is actually speaking. This is called writing from a first person perspective. (Remember in Chapter Three I had my mother tell the ghost story herself.)

I'm going to take my opening paragraph above and play around with it in order to capture the way my dad used to tell stories of working in the foundries. Look at what I've done and then take some time to re-shape your paragraph into a *spoken voice*, first-person opening.

I was young then and just off the road from Seattle.
Strong? I could shovel black sand twelve hours a day with a
butt between my lips and never get winded! I could hold my
own with the toughest sonsabitches in those places, and they
were mean places to work all right. But it was the best job a
guy off the bum with an eighth grade education could find
in Chicago at the time.

Notice how I've used most of the same information from my first paragraph in this second one. The main difference is that I've now written it as I remember my dad telling it. I've tried to capture my dad's speaking voice by using his particular words, phrasing, and expressions: "just off the road," "butt between my lips," "toughest sonsabitches," "and off the bum." How's yours? Have you re-worked your first paragraph into one in which the reader can *hear* a spoken voice? Read it out loud. Does it sound like the voice of the person you remember? Did that person use certain words or expressions that were unique? Might you add any of those to what you've written? Look over the paragraph again and see if you can add anything to make it more authentic.

I think it's important to point out that as we try to capture someone else's spoken voice, especially someone who might have died a long time ago (my dad, for example, died almost a quarter of a century ago), we are engaging in a process of imaginative re-creation. We are engaged in an artistic act. I don't know if my dad ever said those words *exactly* as I wrote them. He most likely did not. Almost certainly he did not. Nevertheless, I know that they capture the spirit of my father and the essence of his language. What I've written is true to my dad, and if he were alive I know that he would agree. That's what we want to strive for as writers: a truthfulness to ourselves and to all that we write about.

Poetry about Photographs

A third way that we can write about photographs is by composing poems that complement them. This is a vital and time-honored practice. Poets often have used photographs and paintings as inspirations for their work. Moreover, poetry allows us to write more than one piece about a particular photograph. In fact I've written seven poems over the years about a single photograph of my mother's First Communion photograph!

Since the best poetry is about concrete things, and since we already have lists of specific nouns, let's see if we can use our lists to write at least a couple of short poems. First, we'll write a form poem, the *cinquain* that we played around with in Chapter Five, and then we'll try a *free verse* poem, the kind of poetry that we'll explore in greater deal in Chapter Eight. Use your list of nouns and photograph and write your cinquain along with me.

My Cinquain

Foundry (one word name of subject)
Dark dangerous (two words describing the subject)
Shoveling straining molding (three "-ing" or action words)
A slow immigrant death (four words that express a feeling about the subject)
Noose (one word that renames the subject)

I hope you see how my cinquain differs from my two previous paragraphs about the photograph. In this case I've focused on the foundry itself, the brutal world in which my father worked, by looking once again very closely at the picture and by using many of the words from my noun list. We probably can write several cinquains about our photographs. As we explored in Chapter Five, they are easy to write. If you want to try another one—or more—go ahead before moving on. Use your dictionary or thesaurus if you're trying to find different words.

Free verse poetry doesn't follow any particular format, and the length of each line doesn't have to be of any particular length. Generally, when we are writing a free verse poem we try to group ideas and images together and pay attention to how each line sounds. We'll discuss this in more detail in Chapter Nine, but let's give it a first go here.

We'll use our photographs and list of nouns to try and capture a particular *image,* and we'll try to do so in a handful of lines or less. Look at my first attempt below before you begin yours.

His scoop shovel upright in the black sand,
Grime-faced partner leaning on an iron rod,
Surrounded by chains, cables, bricks, and girders,
Callused hands curled and hung by his side,
My father stares bravely into the camera.

What I've done is to focus on a specific image: My father in what the English poet William Blake called a "dark satanic mill." I've tried to create this particular image by using the items from my noun list to highlight the brutal conditions of such a working environment. I've kept all five lines about the same length and I've paid attention to how the words and lines sound together. For example, notice the "s" sound in the first line, the "r" sound in the second line, and the way I've used "callused"/"curled" and "hands"/"hung"/"his" in the fourth line. I've used the word "bravely" to describe my father for having to work in such a place.

Using my short poem above as an example, take some of the words from your noun list, add others if needed, and write a short free verse poem which captures some aspect of your photograph. Pay attention to how you might use concrete nouns, sound, and line length to create a particular image. Remember, there's no "right" or "correct" way to write a poem—any poem. And remember, a poem can be of any length. Play around with your words, sounds, and images. That's what poetry is all about: play with language. Give it a go! Play!

Review of What We've Done

In this chapter we've looked at how we might use a valuable and ready-to-hand resource as inspiration for our writing. Photographs help us to remember, to re-create, and to capture our pasts. They encourage us to bring to life again in words people who might be long dead and places we might not have seen in decades. It is in our writing about them that pictures do indeed "say a thousand words."

We've also seen that there are different ways of writing about photographs. We've tried several: describing the photograph; allowing a person in the photograph to speak for him- or herself; and capturing specific aspects of the photograph with short poems, both cinquain and free verse. Making lists of nouns before we write about photographs is often a valuable way of forcing us to look closely at them.

Now, since we've just finished playing around with photographs and poetry, let's turn to Chapter Eight and try our hands at some other kinds of poetry. We'll also look at another common resource that I and many Senior writers have found especially inspirational, and that is music.

Free Poetry

Introduction

We ended Chapter Seven by writing poetry to photographs that we liked, and we wrote a variety of form poetry in Chapter Five. In this chapter we'll explore some other ways of writing poetry. Why another chapter on poetry? As I've discussed before, in my work with Seniors I have found almost all of them were excited about writing poetry once they got over their initial apprehension and saw how much fun it could be. But more than that, poetry often allows us to say what the American poet Donald Hall calls "the unsayable." We find that there are certain things we can only say, or say best, in the poetic form. The English Romantic poet Samuel Taylor Coleridge said the same thing almost two hundred years ago. He maintained that poetry had its roots in our human need for insight and heightened perceptions. He said that poetry was the imaginative expression of an inward knowledge that we best access through the creative act of writing. Let's imaginatively express ourselves by trying our hands at three different kinds of poems: *If I Get Another Life Poems; Metaphor and Simile Poems;* and *Writing Poetry to Music.*

If I Get Another Life Poems

As we age all of us look back over our lives and ask at times, "What if. . . ?" What if we would have chosen one career over another? What if we had not done certain things in our youth? What if we had taken an opportunity offered to us but refused because of our timidity? Poets have explored these "what ifs" in a variety of ways. America's great poet Robert Frost wrote a poem that is known to even those who don't read poetry: "The Road Not Taken." In it he describes how he came to two paths in an autumn wood and decided to take one path and not the other although both paths looked about the same. He goes on to write that in our lives we are constantly coming upon such choices, and each path we take leads us on a particular journey through life. The paths we choose, he concludes, make "all the difference."

Here is a poem by Dorothy Bachman, a member of one of my Senior writing groups. In it she explores Frost's theme of roads taken and not taken in life.

Turnings Not Taken
I have always been afraid to take risks.
I always played the safe side of the street.
What have I missed by stepping carefully
And avoiding the cracks in the sidewalk?
If I had it to do over again I would:
Climb more mountains, ski more slopes,

And toboggan down more hills;
Swim more rivers and hit more golf balls;
Fly more airplanes and ride more roller coasters;
Dive from the highest platforms;
Wear higher heels and dance more polkas.

I love the last line, "Wear higher heels and dance more polkas"!

Similarly, Robert Bly, the contemporary master poet from Minnesota, has written a little poem titled "Clothespins." In it he says that if he had to do it over again he'd like to have spent his life making clothespins. Using Bly's idea of considering what she might do if she had to live her life again, Ardis Kiernan, another member of the Senior writing group in which Dorothy participates, wrote the following poem:

If I Get Another Life. . .
I will be a maker of majestic
Animal kites—kites that
Little people can fly with handles
To keep them from floating away.
They could have tigers, lions,
Zebras and such soaring and dipping,
Climbing high seeing the world
Then returning to their trainers below.
If I should get another life.

Let's Try Writing Our Own Poems

Following the process that we have been using throughout much of the book, let's generate some ideas by brainstorming and listing what we think we might like to do if we get another chance in life. I'll make my list, and you do the same on another piece of paper. Let's think like poets as we brainstorm! We don't have to limit ourselves to literal things, for example, thinking I would be a banker instead of a teacher. Let's be as imaginatively creative as possible by letting our often unexpressed desires surface; think of Ardis above making kites or Dorothy diving from the highest platforms.

My "Another Life" Ideas

Sailboat captain
Bookstore proprietor
Lifeguard for stranded starfish
Mountain guide
Weaver of fine cloth
Cowboy
Resort owner
Hunter of seashells
Baker of Lithuanian rye bread
Newspaper columnist
Juggler in a circus
Ballroom dancer
Gardener of flowers
Owner of an apple orchard
Horse trainer

That's my list. How's yours coming along? As I brainstorm, more and more ideas come into my mind; I can probably list another ten or fifteen things. Notice how my list includes "practical" things such as "bookstore proprietor," and "imaginative" things such as "lifeguard for stranded starfish." Try to include both in your list. After you have listed at least ten or fifteen things for "another life," select one that you first want to write about. We'll then do a second round of brainstorming and listing on that thing.

I'm going to select "resort owner" for my brainstorming and eventual poem. After you have decided on one of yours, let's make our lists together. We can use the Reporter's 5Ws & H if we'd like.

Resort Owner
Owner of a "Mom & Pop" resort (Who)
In northern Wisconsin (Where)
Two Sisters lake
Early summer mornings (When)
Sit on the dock and watch the lake (Why)
Connect to the summer land of my youth
Time to muse on the important things of life
Visit with guests from the cities
Watch sunfish and bass rise (What)
Drift in rowboat with coffee (How)
Feed deer at wood's edge
Clear down trees and split firewood
Cook on a wood burning stove for fun
Be isolated for days in snowstorms and read
Listen to the loons at night
Canoe to beavers' lodges
Play horseshoes with guests
Tell stories to children around the campfire

That's my list of ideas for my "another life" as a resort owner. Once again, I can certainly add more things, but I think this is enough to get me started on a poem. Notice that I identified certain items with the Reporter's 5Ws & H; obviously, I could have done the same thing with all of them. I think we have that strategy pretty much internalized; thus, from now on I'll only make brief mention of it. Once you have a list of things related to your "another life," let's see if we can get a first draft of our poems.

Trying a First Draft

I grew up in the inner-city of Chicago, but every summer our family would travel to the northern woods of Wisconsin where we would stay at one or two small, family-owned resorts. Sometimes my mother and we children would remain for more than a month. For more than fifty years now, I have returned to that particular area of Wisconsin for various lengths of time. My memory teems with fond and vivid images of those resorts, lakes, and forests. The owner of one of the resorts is still actively running it at eighty-five years of age. I think of him as a write this first draft.

Next time around I'll own a resort,
Maybe one on Two Sisters Lake
In the birch and hemlock forest
Of far northern Wisconsin.
I'll rise before dawn and walk
Down to the dock with my coffee
And drift out into the lake
Waiting for the sun to rise.
The gold glitter on the water
And pearls of silver strung along
The lily pads and still reeds
Will be my income for the day.

That's my first attempt. What I've done is to use the ideas I listed along with the memories that emerged in my mind's eye as I began to write, for example, the way I would be fascinated as a kid (and still am as an adult!) with the drops of dew gleaming on the lily pads and reeds along the shore of a lake. As I wrote I also pictured Walter, the resort owner, at eighty-five rowing out into the lake in the morning. I could see myself doing that.

How is your first draft? Have you used your brainstormed list? Did other ideas come into your mind as you began to write? Does your poem paint a picture of sorts? What sort of structure are you using to give your poem some coherence? You might use some sort of rhyme scheme such as we did with rhymed couplets in Chapter Five. Or you might try to build your poem around lines of similar syllable length such as I did: my draft is structured around an eight-syllable line with a few lines of seven and nine syllables.

You might also pay attention to the *sound patterns* of words as you write. That's what I tried to do consciously as I wrote, for example, the "l" sound in the last three lines of my poem or the "dawn," "down," "dock," "drift" pattern I used in the middle. There are various ways to get a "poetic" effect, and no single one is the only "correct" one. Some poems rhyme and some don't. Some have regular lines and some don't. The important thing is the image you are creating. You can always play with your poem by thinking of the *best* words to capture the image you are striving for. The first words that come to mind are not always the best.

Let's both try to make a couple of changes to our first drafts. I'm going to read my poem out loud a couple of times—remember the importance of reading your work out loud!—and see if I can do anything to strengthen it. You do the same with yours. Take your time. Perhaps you might want to put the poem away for the day and return to it later or tomorrow. That's what I'm doing with mine.

Okay, we're back. I let my poem "incubate" overnight, and I think I'm going to try two word changes. I'm going to change "own" in the first line to "run." In the ninth line I'm going to substitute "of" for "on." I think "run" is better than "own" for two reasons. First, I really don't care if I owned the resort or not; I'd simply like to be there, even as an employee. Second, "run" sounds better with "resort" than "own." Changing "of" for "on" might seem insignificant, but it better captures what I'm trying to say, that is, it's the water *itself* that's important to me and not just the times it happens to be gleaming. Here's my altered poem:

Next time around I'll run a resort,
Maybe one on Two Sisters Lake
In the birch and hemlock forest
Of far northern Wisconsin.
I'll rise before dawn and walk
Down to the dock with my coffee
And drift out into the lake
Waiting for the sun to rise.
The gold glitter of the water
And pearls of silver strung along
The lily pads and still reeds
Will be my income for the day.

Have you been able to make any changes in your first draft? Have you read both versions out loud? Do you like the way the second one sounds? Do you have a sharper image? Are you capturing what you want to say in the poem? We can continue to play around with our poems, and I'm going to do so with mine over the next days and weeks. You might want to do the same with yours; however, if you like what you have now, that's fine. Keep it.

Now for some more poetic practice let's both try one more "another life" poem from our first brainstormed lists. Follow the same process we did with this poem. Whenever you're ready we'll move on to the second kind of poetry writing: *Writing Metaphor and Simile Poems.* Here's my second "another life" poem.

Star Baker
I could have been a baker like my dad,
Working rye flour and caraway seeds
Into the butter and egg-rich dough
Beside the men from Lithuania
Who labored long at the wooden counter,
Shaping round loaves into "Star Bakery"
Rye—the best bread this side of the Baltic.

Metaphor and Simile Poems

One of the values of reading and writing poetry, and one of its many pleasures, is the way poetry often startles us with new insights and new ways of seeing things. This is often accomplished by the use of metaphor and simile. Indeed, we might even say that metaphor is the very soul of poetry. A *metaphor* says that something is something else, for example, "He is pig-headed," or "She is a fish in the water." Now the man literally does not have a pig's head, and the woman doesn't grow gills and fins in the water, but comparing these people to these animals gives us an insight into certain aspects of their personalities or physical attributes. We make such comparisons all the time without thinking twice about them. We might even say that as humans we are natural metaphor users.

A *simile* also makes a comparison, but it uses "like" or "as" in doing so. For example, we might say "She is *like* a fish in water," or "She swims as gracefully *as* a fish." Poets also make great use of similes, and we do too in our everyday speech. A simile generally does not have the same power as a metaphor because the comparison being made is explicitly stated. Notice the difference if we take the metaphor from a poem by Emily Dickinson and change it into a simile: "Hope is the thing with feathers/That perches in the soul." Here she is saying that hope *is* a kind of bird. If we turn it into a simile, "Hope is *like* a thing with feathers/That perches in the soul," I hope you see that the power of the image is lessened.

Certainly this does not mean that we should always try to use metaphors and avoid similes. Both are very effective and can help us create interesting poems with memorable lines. For example, some of the most powerful similes can be found in great world religious texts. Take "The Book of Job" from the Old Testament. In it you will find such similes as: "His bones are as strong pieces of brass;/his bones are like bars of iron," and "His heart is as firm as a stone;/yea, as hard as a piece of the nether millstone." Now these are fierce images! In the same section of "Job," however, we also find the poet using such metaphors as this to describe the whale: "His breath kindleth coals,/and a flame goeth out of his mouth." Clearly, the "Job" poet uses both metaphor and simile to great effect. So can we.

Let's Play Around with Similes and Metaphors

Before we try our hands at metaphor and simile poems, let's practice playing around with them. Here are the beginnings of some similes. Take your time and make as many comparisons as you'd like, but try to make at least three for each example before you look at the way I worked with them.

Strong as_____.
Funny as_____.
Grouchy as _____.
Laughs like _____.
Her hair is like_____.

How did it go? I hope making such comparisons through similes is an enjoyable and creative activity for you. Here's what I did:

Strong as an ox/lion/bear/elephant/etc.; as Abraham Lincoln/ my mother; as an oak tree/Mount Rainier; as my memory of you.
Funny as Groucho Marx/Woody Allen/Bob Hope/etc; as a playful puppy; as politicians in Washington.
Grouchy as a baby with colic; as a teenager who broke up with her boyfriend; as a father whose son plays his heavy metal music all day.
Laughs like a hyena/seagull/crow/etc; like a banshee; like a crazy ghost from a horror movie; like the sweet bird songs of spring.
Her hair is like summer wheat; like gossamer; like night; like a mystery to me; like the sea in which I want to drown.

What I've done above is to show how we can control to some extent through our writing the way we have people look at the world. Obviously, there's a dramatic difference between saying that "She laughs like a seagull" and "She laughs like the sweet bird songs of spring"!

Now let's practice by playing around with a few metaphors. What I'd like you to do here is to actually *observe* the thing for which you are creating a metaphor. Thus, you might want to go outside and look at some trees, stand below them, rub your hands over them, and so forth. Once again, take some time to create your metaphors before you see what I did, and try to create at least three for each item. And, of course, take your time.

A tree is _____.
A hand is _____.
The sky is _____.
An apple is _____.

Did you find it easy to create metaphors? The more we play around with them, the more easily we are able to make interesting comparisons. Here's what I did.

A tree is a guardian/sentinel/protector/etc.; Mother Earth's child; an embrace.

A hand is road map; a token of love/hate/etc.; a family of fingers and thumb; a key to your heart.

The sky is an ocean/sea/prairie/etc.; a canvas on which clouds paint pictures; the sun's lover; my heart's home.

An apple is a red ball; a house for worms; a yellow sun; waiting for a coat of caramel and nuts.

As you can see, our metaphors can be "conventional" or more unusual, for example, "An apple is a red ball" compared with "An apple is a house for worms."

Now that we've got into the swing of metaphors and similes, let's try our hands at writing some short poems.

Let's Write Some Simile Poems

I'd like you to go back to the list of "Memorable People" that you generated in Chapter Four. If you have misplaced the list, then you might want to take some time to make another one. Remember in Chapter Four we brainstormed people from our pasts about whom we might want to write. Here's my list from that chapter:

People from our earliest years: parents; grandparents; siblings; other relatives; neighbors who cared for us—I remember my aunt in the next apartment who babysat us; children with whom we played;

People from our childhood: teachers—I remember Sister May Jean Frances from St. Bridget's School; neighborhood or town role models—I remember Mrs. Labney, the honest and kind owner of the local grocery store; school friends; adults with whom we might have worked—I remember the old man I used to help with his garden; people with whom we had brief, but memorable, encounters—I remember the old Black man who used to come through the alleys with his horse and wagon crying "Rags-a-lie!";

People from our young adulthood: high school friends and first loves—I remember dark-haired Carolyn and then tall and blond Barbara in high school; people with whom we worked on a variety of jobs; pastors, ministers, rabbis, and other members of the clergy who might have counseled us;

People after we left home and were on our own: those in the military—I remember Corporal Carleton from boot camp;

friends and teachers at college; colleagues at our first long-term jobs; our future spouse; our own children;

People from our middle years: friends that have remained friends for decades; new acquaintances; important people from our communities; individuals who have caused us to make dramatic changes in the directions of our lives— I remember a professor who said I should pursue an advanced degree;

People from our later years: new friends that we've made, perhaps since we've retired; grandchildren; individuals we've encountered with new interests—I remember Bertha Bess who joined one of my Senior writing groups in southern Illinois

Let's select one person from our lists and write a simile poem about him or her. I'm going to choose Corporal Carleton, one of the drill instructors I had in Marine Corps boot camp. Then together let's make our lists of specific things we remember about the persons.

Corporal Carelton
Tall
Slim
Squinty-eyed
Scar under his left eye
Scar on his chin
Narrow, bony face
Eastern Kentucky dialect
Tough
Did push-ups on his knuckles
Uniforms perfectly creased
Shoes brilliantly polished
Chain-smoked

Called marching cadence that was barely understandable
Was hard on us troopers
Often smell like liquor after a weekend

As I brainstormed my list, Corporal Carelton surfaced again in my mind's eye. I have not really thought about him in over thirty-five years, but now he clearly surfaces. That's what our writing can do for us: it can bring back vividly parts of our past.

Once you have your list (and try to generate at list ten specific things about your memorable person), we will begin to write our short simile poems.

I'm going to take two things from my list and use them to write two specific similes. Here's what I've done:

Face narrow as a flint arrowhead
Scar like a crescent moon on his chin

Now you do the same thing with two of the items from your list. Remember you want to compare some specific things about your person to other things by using "as" or "like." Try to make comparisons that capture the uniqueness of the person. For example, I compared Corporal Carelton's face to a flint arrowhead because I wanted to capture his hardness and rugged features. Once you have your two similes look at the next two that I've written.

Knuckles as callused as old leather
His whisky breath like a message from home

Once again, you write two more similes for your person.

We can continue taking each item from our lists and writing similes; however, a poem of nothing *but* similes would be artificial-sounding and probably not very interesting. Thus, we have to choose when and where we use a simile and when we just describe something in our poems. Let's take one or more of the similes we've just generated and use them as the beginnings for our poems. I'll write mine below, and you start on yours.

Corporal Carleton
Face as hard as a flint arrowhead,
Knuckles on which he did push-ups
Callused as old leather,
Boots that captured the sun
Like deep black mirrors,
His barely intelligible singing
Of cadence in a dialect
Shaped in Kentucky hollers

How's your poem coming? Notice what I've done with this beginning first draft. As I started writing I began to *work with* the similes I have. Thus, "Face as narrow as a flint arrowhead" became "Face as hard as a flint arrowhead." I also added another simile that I think captures his brilliantly polished boots: "Boots that captured the sun/Like deep black mirrors." Notice though that I also simply described his voice and dialect: "Shaped in Kentucky hollers."

Look at what you've written so far. Have you used at least one simile? Is it striking? Might you make a better or different comparison that would be stronger? Have you also included some straightforward description in your poem?

Read what you've written so far out loud. How does it sound? Might you move anything about?

If you'd like at this point, take a break and put away your simile poem until later. If you're "into it" now, however, let's continue.

I'm going to complete my portrait of Corporal Carleton by using a couple more things from my brainstormed list. You do the same with your simile poem. Don't be afraid to use new ideas, images, and similes that come to your mind as you write!

Corporal Carleton

Face as hard as a flint arrowhead,
Knuckles on which he did push-ups
Callused as old leather,
Boots that captured the sun
Like deep black mirrors,
His barely intelligible singing
Of cadence in a dialect
Shaped in Kentucky hollers—
He beat us into the ground.
But the times he came back from town
Red-eyed and sometimes bruised
With the sweet smell of whiskey,
Chain-smoking Camels like my dad,
I grew homesick and imagined
That SOB putting his arm around me.

That's a first draft of my poem. Notice that I make only one more comparison in it: "Chain-smoking Camels like my dad." Obviously what I'm trying to do here is capture the fact that Corporal Carelton was for us 18-year-olds in boot camp a father-figure, one that we resented but at the same time admired.

How's your poem? Have you used items from your brainstormed list? Added any new similes? Have you read your poem out loud? Do you like the way it sounds? What lines or part of your poem do you like best so far? In mine I like "His barely intelligible singing/Of cadence in a dialect/Shaped in Kentucky hollers." I like the way it sounds when I say it out loud, and I like the way it captures something unique about Corporal Carelton, that is, his roots in the mountains of eastern Kentucky. I also like "singing/Of cadence" instead of simply writing that he "called cadence"; "singing" reflects the romantic image of the Marine Corps drill instructor. In all of your writing, whether it is poetry or prose, always try to find something that you especially like and spend a little time examining it. By consciously focusing on the best parts of your writing you will more naturally begin to extend those positive features to all of your other writing.

If you choose, continue to work on your poem, or put it away until later when you might come back to it and do another draft. That's what I'm going to do with mine. Or you might even simply put it away and never come back to it. Remember, that's okay too. We don't have to re-work or like everything we write.

Before we move on to trying our hands at a couple of metaphor poems, let's pick one more person from our memorable person list and write a short simile poem about him or her. Follow our usual procedure: make a list of things about that person; select a couple of them and shape them into similes; add new things or similes as you write and they come to mind; read your developing poem out loud to hear how it sounds; don't be afraid to move words or lines around; and don't be afraid to try unique or striking similes. Here's my second simile poem. It's about Sister Mary Jean Frances, one of my teachers in elementary school. It's short, and notice that I use only one simile: "Only her blue eyes/Like untended spring flowers."

Sister Mary Jean Frances
Her young face framed
In the black-and-white habit,
Only her blue eyes
Like untended spring flowers
And voice that hummed
Popular radio tunes
Gave us children a hint
Of the spirit inside the robe.

Let's Write Some Metaphor Poems

Now that we've written a couple of simile poems, those which utilize metaphors should be easy to construct. Remember that whereas a simile makes an obvious comparison by using "like" or "as," for example, "Her hair is like gossamer," a metaphor makes an implied comparison, for example, "Her hair is gossamer." As I mentioned earlier, both devices are used by poets to great effect. Before we write a couple of new poems, let's see how easy it is to change our simile poems into metaphors by playing around with the poems we just wrote. Here's mine on Corporal Carelton. Take out yours.

Corporal Carleton

Face as hard as a flint arrowhead,
Knuckles on which he did push-ups
Callused as old leather,
Boots that captured the sun
Like deep black mirrors,
His barely intelligible singing
Of cadence in a dialect
Shaped in Kentucky hollers—
He beat us into the ground.
But the times he came back from town
Red-eyed and sometimes bruised
With the sweet smell of whiskey,
Chain-smoking Camels like my dad,
I grew homesick and imagined
That SOB putting his arm around me.

I'm going to change the first three similes I used into metaphors. Before you play around with your poem, see what I've done.

Corporal Carleton

Face a flint arrowhead,
Knuckles on which he did push-ups
Callused old leather,
Boots that captured the sun
Deep black mirrors,
His barely intelligible singing
Of cadence in a dialect
Shaped in Kentucky hollers—
He beat us into the ground.
But the times he came back from town

Red-eyed and sometimes bruised
With the sweet smell of whiskey,
Chain-smoking Camels like my dad,
I grew homesick and imagined
That SOB putting his arm around me.

Notice that I've turned the similes into metaphors: "Face a flint arrowhead"; knuckles are now "Callused old leather"; and the boots are now "Deep black mirrors." I didn't change the last simile, "Chain-smoking Camels like my Dad," because I think that line works best as it is. However, I think "Face a flint arrowhead" is much more powerful and immediate than "Face as hard as a flint arrowhead"; it emphasizes the corporal's toughness and sharpness.

Play around with the similes in your poem. See if you can turn them into metaphors. Which do you like better, the similes or metaphors? And then just for fun let's do the same thing with our second poems. Here's my changed poem on Sister Mary Jean Frances.

Sister Mary Jean Frances
Her young face framed
In the black-and-white habit,
Only her blue eyes
Untended spring flowers,
And voice that hummed
Popular radio tunes
Gave us children a hint
Of the spirit inside the robe.

I like "Untended spring flowers" better than "Like untended spring flowers." It captures the underlying spirit and willfulness of the young nun.

Before we move on, let's try another use of metaphor by writing a short, three or four line, metaphor poem about ourselves. Let's fool around and try to describe ourselves in a humorous manner. Select an animal, plant, or other thing that you might compare yourself to in a funny way. I'm going to compare myself to an herb plant—dill weed. Let's think about ourselves and how the particular animals, plants, or things might say something about our personalities.

I as a Dill Weed

Spindly
Spreads uncontrollably
Feathery leaves
Unique seeds
Sways in the wind
Seeds ready in the late summer

Do you have a list of things that describe the animal, plant, or thing to which you're going to compare yourself in a humorous manner? Okay, now let's take a couple of those and create metaphors to comment upon our own personalities, foibles, or idiosyncrasies. Let's be funny in a few lines! Here's mine.

The Dill Weed

Spindly shanks dancing,
Head full of feathery thoughts
Spreading uninvited,
The seeds good for sauerkraut.

People who know me who agree with this metaphor self-portrait!

Let's Write Poetry to Music

Music and poetry just naturally seem to go together. Many kinds of music can stir in our imaginations vivid pictures of different settings, people, and things. I have found with Seniors, and with much younger writers, that classical music and jazz are especially good in calling forth in the mind's eye images which can then be transformed into poetry. Here are a couple of short poems written by Seniors after they listened to Debussy's "La Mer":

To Me
Beautiful music is like a warm summer breeze
Coming in from the sea
Into an open window
Blowing the curtains
And soothing my restless soul.

Soft Music
by Douglas Nielsen
Soft music and waltzes
Are made to create memories
Of togetherness, love, contentment,
And a feeling of wanting
That I have still.

Different pieces of music will result in different kinds of poems. "La Mer," or the sea, calls forth these kinds of soft, quiet, and meditative poems. After listening to some

Dixieland jazz, Dorothy Bachman wrote a long poem titled "Music." Here is one stanza from that poem. You can see how she "got into" it!

> . . . *Then there is the naughty side of my soul*
> *That causes me to think in a past life*
> *I must have been a dancehall girl.*
> *I love the fun and raunchy tempo*
> *Of striptease music, "Hello Dolly" tunes,*
> *Country square dance music and the polka.*

Let's play around with some music and see what kinds of poetry we might write in response to it. You'll have to select a piece of music for this writing activity, one that you have on a record, tape, or CD and that you can replay. Pick an instrumental piece, something without lyrics; it might be classical, dance music, jazz, or something from a musical. While you're playing the music, I'd like you to do the following:

1) Close your eyes and listen.
2) How does the music make you feel?
3) What does the music remind you of?
4) What does the music make you see?
5) What colors do you see?

Okay? Once you have selected your piece of music, let's listen. I'm going to listen to a slow jazz piece by Duke Ellington and John Coltrane titled "My Little Brown Book."

Now that we've listened to our respective pieces of music, let's listen to them again. Are you feeling the same things you did during the first playing? Are you reminded of anything new? What are you seeing now? What about colors?

Gathering Ideas and Images

Now that we've listened to the music a couple of times, let's brainstorm and list some words and images that the music called forth and which we might use in our poems. As usual, I'll ask you to follow along with me on a new sheet of paper.

Colors I Saw
Misty blues
Amber light from table lamps
Dark gray shadows
White vapors from cigarette smoke
Hues of brown from the musicians' faces

What I Was Reminded Of
Jazz club in Norway
Blues club in Chicago
"Casablanca": Rick's Café
Thin, dangerous men with fedoras
Lovely, long-legged women
A couple staring at each other over a bottle of champagne
Manhattan skyline

How are your lists coming? If you are having trouble generating your lists, close your eyes and listen to the music again. Notice also how I am trying to capture *specific* images, particular things that I see. Let's continue listing.

What I Felt
Lazy—but with a kind of sleepy energy
Nostalgic over lost loves
Romantic—wanting to put on a tux and dance like Fred Astaire
Wistful thinking of long-gone bars and cafes I once knew

Let's Use Our Lists and Write Short Poems

Now that we have our lists we can use them to play around with the words and images to create short poems. Remember, poems don't have to be long, and they don't necessarily have to rhyme. As we're writing our poems, we can always go back and listen to our pieces of music for further inspiration. To begin, let's try a simple two or three line poem that captures a single image. Look over your list and see what things you might put together to create such an image. Here's what I'm going to try from my lists:

The white trails of cigarette smoke
Rise above the young couple
Staring into each other's eyes

And a second attempt

The bronze face of the saxophone player
Glistens under the dim amber light

Do you see what I'm doing? I'm simply taking items from my lists and playing around with them to create single images. Notice that as I'm using the words and images in my lists, other—and I think better—words come to mind. So instead of writing "vapors" of cigarette smoke I used "trails," and instead of "hues of brown" I used "bronze." As I've said before, the more we play around with words and language, the more adept we become at finding different words and images.

Have you created one or more short poems from your lists? Does your poem or do your poems capture a specific image? I'm going to write another short one from my lists, and then I'd like you to do the same. Afterwards, I'd like you to put this chapter away and come back to it later, perhaps tomorrow or the first chance you get after that.

Here's my third short poem:

From out of the dark gray shadows
Ingrid Bergman's face
Lights up Rick's Café

Let's Listen Again and Try a Longer Poem

Welcome back! I hope you've let this poetry writing from music lie fallow for a day or so. I know I have. Let's review what we've done with our particular pieces of music and our poems. First, read over the lists you generated after listening to your piece of music. Second, read your poems out loud. Do you still like them? Is there anything you might change to make them stronger, that is, to help them capture specific images related to the music? And now, third, let's go back and listen to our respective pieces of music one more time; this will bring them back to us in a fresh manner. Remember to keep your eyes closed as you are listening.

As I closed my eyes and listened again to Duke Ellington and John Coltrane's "My Little Brown Book," I saw and felt many of the same things as before. However, this time I also saw clearly a young woman in her early twenties dancing all alone in the middle of the small dance floor. Here is a list of my new images, feelings, and colors.

New Things & Colors I Saw and Felt

Very tiny dance floor in front of jazz quartet

A young woman dancing alone with closed eyes, swaying to the music

She is tall and slim in black slacks and blouse
Her short hair is dyed an electric purple
She has large gold earrings dangling from her ears and a dia-
mond stud glittering in her nostril
Everyone in the club is watching her
She is the fixed star that captures both the music and our long-
ings

Those are some of the new things I saw as I listened again to the music. You will find that each time you listen to any piece of music you will almost always see something new. That's why writing about music is so much fun: We can continue, if we so choose, to write several poems or vignettes about the same piece. Let's try that now. I'm going to look over my original lists and the short poems I wrote and see if I can write a longer poem which incorporates some of the things from my new list. You do the same. Remember that your poem doesn't have to rhyme, but it might, and that you want to try to create some vivid images. Here's my longer poem:

White trails of cigarette smoke
Curl above the young
Long-legged woman
With electric-purple hair
As she sways alone
With closed eyes and smile
On the tiny wooden floor
In front of the quartet
Her gold earrings glisten
Under the dim amber light
And we follow her our star
In the early-morning hours

That's a first draft of a longer poem. I can continue to play around with it if I choose. You can see how I used lines and images from my original lists and short poems and connected them to things in my new list. This new poem is different than the shorter ones that I wrote earlier. How is your new poem? Were you able to use anything from your first lists? Were you able to incorporate lines or images from your short poems? The more you play around with what you have brainstormed and captured on paper, I'm sure the more possibilities you will see.

Review of What We've Done

In this chapter we've looked at three different ways of writing poetry: writing about what we might do if we got another life in which to do it; using similes and metaphors to create unique and striking comparisons; and writing poetry to music. We have spent time with these forms of poetry because they, along with the form poetry we wrote in Chapter Five, can help us look closely at our writing, at how we choose and use words, images, and ideas. Even if we'd rather write in prose, playing around with poetry in general and with similes and metaphors in particular will help us become more confident and skillful writers. I encourage you to continue to try your hand at poetry on a regular basis. Now let's move on to our next chapter and explore how we might use our own lives and experiences as a basis for writing fiction.

CHAPTER NINE

Fiction

Introduction

I have found in my work with Seniors that writing fiction is a pleasurable and engaging activity. We are all natural born storytellers, and we enjoy telling stories and hearing those of others. Fiction is storytelling par excellence, and the writing of it allows us to do three main things. First, it enables us to imaginatively create unique characters, situations, and events. It allows us to be "world makers." Second, by using our own lives and experiences as a basis for fiction, we can often explore and play around with "what ifs," for example: "What if I didn't take that summer trip to the Grand Canyon but instead went to Venice, Italy?" or "What if I met a troubled artist at a café in St. Mark's Plaza, and she asked me to accompany her to Rome?" Third, by fictionalizing our lives we sometimes are able to write about past experiences that otherwise would be too disturbing or hurtful to explore. Fictionalizing our pasts helps us to gain some emotional distance from them. Let's begin by looking at some elements of stories.

Elements of Story

Most good stories, whether they are the ones we tell or read in the form of a novel or a short story, have certain key elements or ingredients. Let's review them before we move on to trying our hands at writing a short piece of fiction. We've already briefly explored *character, setting,* and *action* in Chapter Seven on writing about photographs.

Character

A story will always involve one or more characters. These may be humans, animals, mythical beings, science fiction creatures, or others. Typically, at least one of the characters will be central, that is, he or she will be "dynamic" and will somehow grow or change in the course of the story. We get a deeper insight into this character than into the others we encounter.

Setting

A story of course takes place in some particular context and at some particular time, and this is called the setting. There might be more than one setting in a story, for example, my childhood neighborhood in Chicago in the 1950s and the rustic resort in Wisconsin at which we stayed in the summer of 1960. The story might be an actual place, for example, Wendt's Resort in northern Wisconsin, or it might be an imaginary one, for example, an old lumberjack's homestead outside of Lake Tomahawk, Wisconsin.

Plot

The plot of a story is the action, or what happens. Sometimes in a story we begin at the very beginning, "Once upon a time," and then proceed to tell it chronologically from beginning through the middle to the end. However, we can also start a story in the middle and then proceed to tell it by going backwards and forwards in time. Or we can even tell a story by beginning at the end and then telling everything that led up to that particular ending.

In order for a story to be interesting there has to be some sort of *conflict,* that is, some sort of problem that involves the characters in the setting. Conflict is what drives the plot along; without a conflict a story might be uninteresting.

Typically a plot will begin with some *steady state* of things, for example, think of the tale of "Little Red Riding Hood." The little girl is sent by her mother to visit her ailing grandmother. Then this steady state is disrupted by the conflict, for example, the big bad wolf eats the grandmother and tries to eat Red Riding Hood. Finally, the conflict is brought to some *resolution,* and things return to a steady state, for example, the wolf is killed by a hunter, and the grandmother and Red Riding Hood are safe once again. The plot of a story might have more than one of these chains of *steady state—conflict—resolution* in it.

Here's a little story by Della Baker, a member of one of my writing groups. In it she elaborates—fictionalizes—a story about her great-grandparents.

When Old Sol Was Found Wanting

My great-grandfather was a strong-minded farmer. He didn't believe in coddling his womenfolk. He would perform the tasks that needed to be performed, but in his own time frame.

One morning great-grandmother reminded him as she handed him his lunch about the need for firewood for the kitchen stove.

"Women, they always want something," he thought. "I'll get it later."

As the problems of the day increased, he forgot about the firewood, sure that there must be enough for one more day.

He was happy to see the sun getting ready to set as he walked home. There was grandmother, his little woman, sitting on the back steps and waiting to greet him.

As he came near, he saw she was surrounded by pans. Peeled potatoes were in a large pan; pork chops in a spider; and freshly shelled peas in a small pan. Off to the side were two cake pans with unborn dough in them.

Now great-grandfather may have been a chauvinist, but dumb he was not. He passed the porch without a word, returning with his arms full of fire wood and a sheepish grin on his face.

He said, "The sun wasn't hot enough, was it, Pet?"

In this brief and witty story (Della said most of it is "made up," that is, fictionalized) we can find all of the elements that I've just described above. Della's great-grandmother and great-grandfather are the *characters,* and in Della's writing of this story we get some insight into the personalities of each. The *setting* is the farmhouse. The *plot* is a chronological one; it begins in the morning and ends as the sun is setting. The *conflict* entails the great-grandfather's failure to do his chore and the great-grandmother's not-so-subtle rebuke. The *resolution* occurs when the great-grandfather gets the wood and tries to save face by joking with his wife. Thus, we can see how this particular *steady state—conflict—resolution— steady state* chain works in the story.

Let's Write Fiction

Before we begin a new piece of fiction, let's play around with something we've already written, and that is, the personal vignettes we wrote in Chapter Six. Take out your vignette and re-read it. Here's mine:

> *On my right forearm is a round scar about the size of a dime. I burned it into my skin when I was sixteen and hanging out on the street corners of Chicago. It has faded during the last forty-odd years and is hard to see now.*
>
> *My buddies and I thought we were "tough guys." Sometimes when we drank too much beer and our girlfriends were around, we'd try to prove our manhood by challenging one another to a game of "chicken" with a cigarette.*
>
> *The game went like this. Two of us would put our forearms together, and one of our girlfriends would light a fresh cigarette and place it between our arms. The first person to jerk away his arm was the "chicken."*
>
> *Oftentimes a whole cigarette would burn out without either person pulling away. Our wide-eyed girlfriends thought we were tough guys.*

It's easy to turn a biographical vignette into a brief fictional story if we pay attention to the elements of character, setting, and plot (steady state—conflict—resolution). Let's identify those elements in our respective vignettes. I'll list mine below, and you do the same with yours on another sheet of paper.

Characters
My teenage buddies, girlfriends, and I

Setting
Late-1950s in inner-city Chicago

Plot
Begins at the end—a scar acquired 40 years ago—and then describes how it was gotten

Conflict
Teenage attempts to prove our manhood

Steady State—Conflict—Resolution—Steady State Chain
Hanging out on the street corner; challenge with cigarette; burning our arms until one or neither pulls away; manhood proven and once again hanging out on the corner

Do you see how I've identified the key elements in my story? I hope you were able to do the same with your personal vignette. Now let's simply play around with those elements and change our vignettes into fictional works. I'm going to do so by re-working my first paragraph and focusing on characters and setting. Here's what I've done.

> *On Richie's right forearm is a round scar about the size of a dime. He burned it into his skin in 1959 when he was sixteen and hanging out on the street corners of Chicago. It has faded during the last forty-odd years and is hard to see now, but if he rolls up his shirtsleeve and separates the dark hair on his arm it is still noticeable.*

Notice how I've simply substituted "Richie" for myself, elaborated on the setting by specifying "1959," and added more descriptive details ("rolls up his shirtsleeves," and so on). Now I'd like you to do the same thing with the beginning of your personal vignette. Transform it into a fictional story by playing with one or more of the basic elements. Once you have done so, let's continue below.

I'm going to re-work the rest of my vignette now by focusing on the plot (steady state—conflict—resolution—steady state chain). Before you continue with yours, look at what I've done.

> *Richie and his buddies thought they were "tough guys."*
> *One hot and humid summer evening when they had drunk*
> *too many quarts of Nectar beer and were trying to impress*
> *both themselves and their girlfriends, Richie challenged Tom*
> *Pirocki to a game of chicken.*
>
> *All of the guys and gals formed a circle around Richie*
> *and Tom as they pressed their arms together. Then Richie's*
> *girlfriend, Barbara, lit a Lucky Strike and carefully placed*
> *it between their forearms. The smell of seared flesh and burnt*
> *hair arose in the night air.*
>
> *No one uttered a sound as Richie and Tom grimaced*
> *and stared at each other. The cigarette slowly burned down to*
> *the end, and neither young man flinched or "chickened out."*
>
> *Everyone cheered, and Richie and Tom grinned at each*
> *other. Barbara threw her arms around Richie and kissed him*
> *while Tom opened another quart of beer and took a long drink..*
>
> *They all wondered what they might do next.*

Notice how I've rewritten my personal vignette by adding specific characters (Tom and Barbara), making the conflict more dramatic (everyone silently watching), adding details (seared flesh, both young men grimacing, and so on), and highlighting the ritual nature of this action (Barbara kissing Richie who has proven himself to be a real "man"). Notice also how the story moves from a steady state to a conflict to a resolution to a new steady state.

Another element of fiction is the *voice* in which the story is told. My personal vignette was told in the "first person," that is, I used "I" in telling the story. The fictionalized version of the story is told in the "third person," that is, I wrote *about* the characters using "he" and "they." We can use either first or third person when writing a fictional story. Obviously, if we are writing about our own experiences, using the third person gives us more emotional distance from ourselves.

I'd like you to re-read what I've written and to compare it to my original vignette. Consider how I played around with the key elements of story to transform a personal memory into a very short fictional piece. Then I'd like you to work with your own vignette. Return to this section when you have completed a draft of your story. Take your time, whether hours, days, or even weeks.

Let's Write More Fiction

I'm going to review again my list of possible topics from Chapter Six. Take out yours again and look it over. Here's mine:

Stories of "firsts," for example: first day in school, first date, first heartbreak, first job, and so on;

Stories of work: best job, worst job;

Stories and family expressions told by parents, grandparents, and other family members;

Stories of childhood or teenage adventures;

Stories about scary experiences, for example, a brush with death;

Stories about "forks" in your life's road;

Stories about "where you were," for example: when World War II ended, when the astronauts landed on the moon, when the millennium began on January 1, 2000, and so forth;

Stories about special places;

Stories about memorable people;

Stories about doing something or making something, for example: canoeing in the Minnesota Boundary Waters Canoe Area Wilderness, walking across the Golden Gate Bridge, giving birth to a set of twins, rebuilding the engine on your first car, and so on;

Stories about how something came to be, for example: how your relatives first came to America, how you got your name, and so forth;

Stories about funny, witty, strange, or sad conversations you overheard or in which you participated.

For this fictional story I'm going to use an experience my brother Ed and I had over twenty-five years ago while on a trip to the Minnesota Boundary Waters Canoe Area Wilderness (BWCA). Briefly, we were staying at a friend's little shack and went out deep into the forest to look for moose. We took a compass along, but in the ensuing rain it got wet and we lost our way. We wandered around the woods for a couple of hours in the cold and rain until we finally found a road and were able to make our way back to the cabin. When we got there we were so cold and so close to suffering from hypothermia that we couldn't turn the key in the padlock on the cabin door. We struggled for more than ten minutes before with great effort we got it open.

I'd like you to select one possible experience from your list of topics about which you might create a fictional short story. Perhaps you have another idea that is not on your list, and that's fine too. As I've said many times already, the more we write and the more we think about our pasts, the more ideas we have. (Be sure to always jot down these ideas in your notebook for future reference! If you're like me, it's easy to forget a great idea unless it's written down.) Once you have the experience or topic you'd like to fictionalize, let's list the key elements of story. I'll list mine below, and you list yours on another piece of paper.

Characters
My brother Ed and I

Setting
Northern Minnesota woods in 1974

Plot
Chronological—from our leaving the shack until we returned

Conflict
Lost in the woods and possible hypothermia

Steady State—Conflict—Resolution—Steady State Chain
Left shack to look for moose; got lost in the rain and cold because of failed compass; wandered for two hours until we found a road and the shack; warm and safe around the pot-bellied stove

Voice
I tell this brief story in the first person, that is, I use "I" and "we"

Do you have your list of story elements? Don't continue until you do. Review mine above if you're having problems.

I'm going to play around with this little story and fictionalize it by making the events more dramatic than they
were and by making it much more descriptive. In order to
brainstorm possible ideas, I'm going to use the visual mapping technique that we tried in Chapters Six and Seven.
Why don't you do the same on another piece of paper.

Lost in the Woods

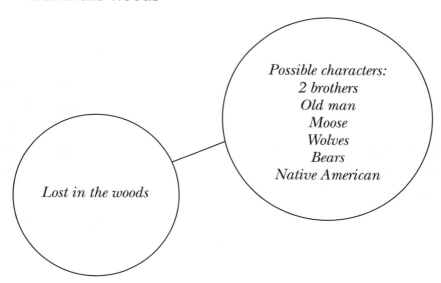

What I've done in this first visual map is to brainstorm
some possible characters who might appear in my fictional
story. I don't know if I'll use all of them, but I want to have
an ample list from which to work. On your piece of paper
I'd like you to begin your visual map by focusing on possible
characters in your story. Once you have that, let's continue
below with possible settings.

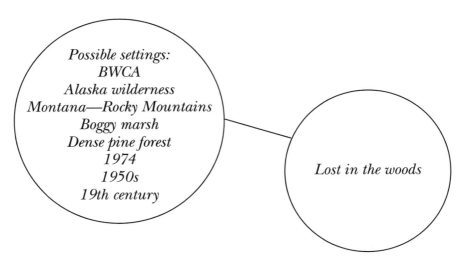

Notice in my visual map that I've brainstormed far beyond the woods of northern Minnesota. I've also thought about more *specific* aspects of the possible setting, for example, the marsh and pine forest and other possible time periods. As you are making your visual map, don't be afraid to list your most "far out" ideas. Quite often what seems at first to be silly later turns out to be the most interesting idea. Now let's do the same thing for possible conflicts.

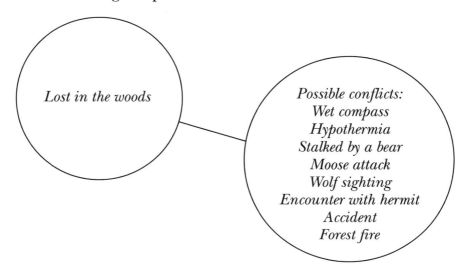

Notice that I've begun with what my brother and I actually experienced, that is, losing our way because of a rain-soaked compass and then approaching a state of hypothermia, but then I've brainstormed other possible things that might have happened. I'm imaginatively constructing other scenarios; I'm moving to a fictional story. Try to brainstorm and list at least another five or six possible conflicts for your story. Then let's each make the last arm of our visual map, and that is possible resolutions.

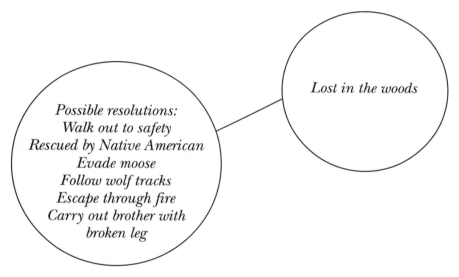

Lost in the woods

Possible resolutions:
Walk out to safety
Rescued by Native American
Evade moose
Follow wolf tracks
Escape through fire
Carry out brother with broken leg

If we now connect all of the arms of our visual map, we can get an idea of the many possibilities for a fictional story. Look below at mine for some examples. From the true life account of how my brother and I got lost in the northern Minnesota woods because of a wet compass, I can now transform that experience into such stories as: Two brothers in Montana in 1953 are attacked by a grizzly bear and are saved by a Native American hunter who shoots the animal; two brothers are trapped in a forest fire but find their way to safety by following the tracks of a wolf pack; two brothers, one

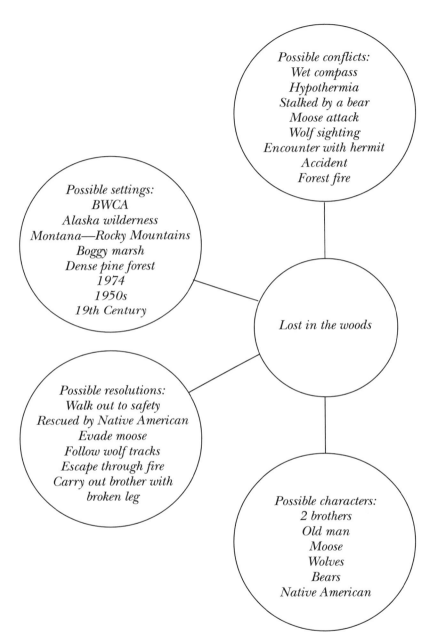

Possible conflicts:
Wet compass
Hypothermia
Stalked by a bear
Moose attack
Wolf sighting
Encounter with hermit
Accident
Forest fire

Possible settings:
BWCA
Alaska wilderness
Montana—Rocky Mountains
Boggy marsh
Dense pine forest
1974
1950s
19th Century

Lost in the woods

Possible resolutions:
Walk out to safety
Rescued by Native American
Evade moose
Follow wolf tracks
Escape through fire
Carry out brother with broken leg

Possible characters:
2 brothers
Old man
Moose
Wolves
Bears
Native American

with a broken leg, encounter a strange hermit in the Alaska wilderness, and he helps them get to a hospital; two brothers in the 1880s are attacked by a moose in a pine forest of Minnesota, but they escape and walk out to safety. And so on.

I hope you can see that by looking at the visual map I can construct various combinations with which to begin my story. Let me point out however that such combinations will only be the *beginnings* to stories. Once we start writing a piece of fiction, the work often takes on "a life of its own." Suddenly, the story that begins with two brothers trapped in a forest fire might end up being about two teenage girls canoeing down a wild white-water river. (And that's no exaggeration!) The important thing is to have a beginning place, something that can get you going, and a visual map provides that starting point. Then it's necessary to be open to the story that unfolds as you write it. Once you start writing fictional pieces, you'll certainly experience what I'm describing here.

Before we continue, I'd like you to put together all of the "arms" to your visual map. Look it over and add to it if new ideas come to mind. Then I'd like you to play around with some possible combinations of characters—settings—conflicts—resolutions in the same manner that I did above. Think of at least four or five different possibilities. We'll continue once you have your completed visual map and some possible ideas for stories. Take your time with this. You might want to come back later after you've had some time to mull over ideas.

Starting Our Stories

Let's begin with one of our combinations. I'm going to write my story about two brothers, ages ten and twelve, who get lost in a northern Minnesota forest in the 1950s and are attacked by a bull moose. They are eventually rescued by an old hermit-lumberjack who lives in a ramshackle log cabin. Now, select the combination with which you'd like to begin.

We've discussed several times the importance of an opening sentence and paragraph to any piece of writing; we want to capture the reader's attention. This is especially true of a fictional piece. Thus, let's each try three different sentences with which to begin our stories. I'll do mine below, and you write yours on another piece of paper.

> *They should have listened to their mother, and now they were lost.*
> *"We're lost," I admitted.*
> *"We should have listened to Mom!" my brother Bobby cried.*
> *After wandering for hours in what seemed to be circles, they knew they were lost.*

There are three possibilities; of course, I could have written many more. Once again, I want to emphasize the importance of trying out options, of not simply selecting the first thing that comes to mind. Do you have at least three different openings? Fine. Let's look at what we've done and then select one with which to begin.

The *voice* in my first and third sentences is the third person, that is, I am writing *about* the boys. In the second sentence I am using the first person, that is, I am writing from the perspective of the character: "I admitted." Typically, but not always, the first person makes the story more personal: as a reader we have the author speaking directly to us. I've decided to write this short story in the first person, and thus I'm going to begin with the second sentence. I also like this opening because the dialogue between the two speakers makes the situation of being lost immediate and dramatic.

Look at your three opening sentences. In what voice is each written? Which one do you like best? Why? Reflect on your choice. Then select one that you'd like to use as the basis for your story.

Now let's each use our particular openings to build a beginning paragraph or perhaps a couple of paragraphs. Remembering what we've explored in previous chapters, we'll try to use specific and descriptive language while keeping in mind that less is often more. We don't have to write a great deal to tell a good story. Give it a go!

> *"We're lost," I admitted.*
> *"We should have listened to Mom!" my brother Bobby cried.*
> *We had been wandering in the woods looking for a trail, and now we were standing next to the same lightning-scarred pine we had passed two hours before. We were walking in circles.*
> *"Whatta we gonna do?" Bobby asked as he slapped at the mosquitoes hovering around his head. His face was covered with splotches of blood, and I was sure that mine looked the same from all of the mosquitoes I had been killing.*
> *"I don't know," I said, "but let's stop and think before we go walking in circles again."*

That's the beginning to my story. I'll point out what I'm trying to do in this draft. First, I'm using dialogue between the two brothers and vernacular English: "Whatta we gonna do?" Second, I'm trying to develop a sense of desperation bordering on panic by highlighting how the boys are being pursued by the mosquitoes: "face covered with splotches of blood." And third, I'm using specific language: "lightning-scarred pine." This is only a first draft, and I might change all of this in subsequent drafts; however, I'm actively *thinking about* what I'm writing as I make word and sentence choices.

How is your beginning? Are you taking the reader into the setting? Giving the reader a sense of the character(s)? Could you possibly use more descriptive or powerful language? Are you being *too* wordy? Is there something you might condense? If you're using dialogue, does it sound natural? Read what you have out loud and see how it all sounds. Once you've reflected on your beginning, let's both continue with our stories.

> *Bobby was right. We should have listened to Mom. She warned us not to stray beyond the shore of the lake and into the woods. She said we were surrounded by a wilderness area and that there were no roads or houses.*
>
> *But we didn't listen. We figured the woods of northern Minnesota couldn't be too deep or wild, so we just tromped along imagining we were hunters or explorers. After a while we got hungry and tried to find our way back, and that's when we knew we were lost.*
>
> *"Whatta we gonna do?" Bobby asked again, and I knew he was ready to cry. He was ten and scared. Although I was only two years older and just as scared, I knew Bobby expected me to find a way home. I was the big brother.*

Time for a Break?

Is your story unfolding for you? You might be discovering that as you write other ideas come into your mind, possibly for other stories. Don't forget to jot those ideas down some-where; you might use them later. Stories beget other stories. Sometimes, however, you might find that you're stuck and don't know where to go with your story. That's only natural, too. If that happens while you're writing, try one of two things. First, simply continue to write, whether what you're writing seems good or not; often we can "write our way out" of a block. Second, put away the piece you're working on and come back to it later; sometimes letting ideas incubate is the best thing to do. Let's continue with our stories now or come back to them later.

> *"The sun set right over our cabin last night," I said, "so that means we've gotta walk west. And that's the way the sun is falling through the trees over there. So let's walk straight in that direction."*
>
> *We followed the setting sun for about a half hour, and we both felt better knowing that we were doing something that seemed to make sense and not just wandering around. We were hoping that soon we'd hear Mom and Dad calling for us.*
>
> *Suddenly as we walked through a thicket of brushy trees and boggy ground we came face to face with a bull moose. It was huge and standing directly in front of us, no more than 30 feet away. Its long face looked like some kind of boulder, and the rack of antlers that arose from its head looked like trees growing out of the stone.*
>
> *We stood there staring at the moose, and it stood there watching us. Then it lowered its head and made a bugling kind of sound. We panicked and began to run in the oppo-site direction. We heard the moose's heavy trot behind us.*

We ran and stood behind a large white pine, and the moose stopped on the other side of the tree, snorting and shaking its head. Bobby and I stayed glued to the tree. We didn't know what to do and were too tired now to run any further.

I don't know what might have happened to us, but the next thing we heard was a rifle shot and a man's voice shouting, "G'on, ya big walkin' hat rack! Get outta here!"

Let's stop here and review what we've done up to now. I'll use the piece I'm writing as an example to point out the elements of story that we explored at the beginning of this chapter.

The *characters* in my story include the narrator, Bobby, the moose, and the person who chases away the moose. The *setting* is in the forest of northern Minnesota. We don't know the time period yet. The *voice* is in the first person. The *plot* involves two brothers getting lost in the woods, being chased by a moose, being rescued, and. . . . We don't know yet what will finally happen. The *conflict* that drives the plot along includes the boys being lost and being chased by a moose. The *resolution*, at least up to this point, involves the boys being rescued by someone.

Look at your story. See if you can identify the same elements in it. Are you able to see the *steady state—conflict—resolution—steady state* chain (or chains) that will eventually form the structure of your story? Notice how I try to create some dramatic tension in my resolution by introducing the man's voice and rifle shot but not the man himself yet. Okay, let's continue with our respective stories.

The moose turned and crashed through the brush and then disappeared into the forest. A man dressed in army fatigues and carrying a rifle emerged from the trees behind us. He was short, stocky, and had a scraggly red beard. He looked to be in his 30s or maybe early-40s.

"What're you kids doing out here?" he growled.

"We're lost!" Bobby said and then began to cry.

I held his hand and was ready to cry myself. "We're staying at Johannsen's Resort, and we were exploring in the woods and got lost."

"Explorin' in the woods. . . bah! You city kids don't know your ass from your elbow when it comes to the woods. Explorin'. . . ."

He came up to us and put his hand on Bobby's shoulder. "It's okay, kid, you're all right now."

The hand on Bobby's shoulder looked like a piece of bark or leather. The faded name sewn on his fatigue shirt was "Olsen." I saw that a long ugly scar came out of his beard, curved up his right cheek, and ended in his eye. There was no life in the eye; it was glass.

"The old eye's somethin', ain't it?" he smiled. "Lost it and got this in Okinawa ten years ago," he said running his hand along the scar. "Two days before we secured the island and I get a piece of a mortar round in my face. I wish they would've dropped a A-bomb on that damn island first."

Notice what I'm doing here. I'm trying to create a brief portrait of the man and at the same time to indirectly state the time period: He got the scar in combat ten years before in the battle for the island of Okinawa. Thus, we know that this story is taking place around 1955 or so.

"My uncles were in the war too," I said.

"Yeah, well, I guess a lot of us were," he grimaced. "My name's Bud, Bud Olsen. Been livin' out here loggin' and what not since I got back from the veteran's hospital in Chicago. Don't have much use for the town and people who sent me over there in the first place. Come on, I'll take you city boys back to the resort. Your folks are probably wonderin' where you are."

He slung his rifle over his shoulder and took hold of Bobby's hand. I held Bobby's other hand, and we walked through the forest as the sun sank lower.

"Don't you ever get lonely out here?" I asked.

"Lonely for what?" he sneered. "Lonely for people starin' at my face, lonely for people feelin' sorry for me, lonely for all of the babble about what I hero I was? Naw, I'm not lonely for all of that."

"But you must miss some people," Bobby said. "Your folks, or a girlfriend, or somebody ."

"Naw, little fella, naw," Bud whispered as we walked along.

We were only a 20 minute hike from the resort. Bobby and I probably had been wandering around it all the time. When we came to the lake shore we saw our cabin across the little bay and then saw and heard Mom and Dad waving and hollering at us.

"You're okay now," Bud said. "There's your folks. You can go on your own from here."

"Why don't you come to our cabin and have something to eat," I said, "or maybe have a beer with my dad. I know they'd want to thank you for finding us."

"Naw, that's okay, I don't mix too well," he said. "You boys just watch yourselves out here. Old Bud might not be

around the next time," he smiled, rubbed our heads, and then walked back into the forest.

I saw Mom and Dad coming along the shore trail to meet us, and I was happy we were home safe and sound. But I was also sad. In my mind's eye I saw Bud walking through the darkening forest to his cabin, touching the scar along his face, and looking out at the world through a single eye.

That's a first draft to my story. I hope you see that as I was writing it, the story began to change. Ostensibly, it's still about the two brothers getting lost, and so forth, but as I introduced the character of the scarred war veteran he took on a life of his own. Now there's another dimension to the story. And, if I so choose, I can write a continuation to this story or perhaps another one about Bud, the hermit-veteran with the one eye.

Do you have a draft to your story? Do you see how it perhaps might lead to more stories? If you'd like, work on a second draft, or even begin a new fictional piece. I think you'll find that writing fiction is not only fun but imaginatively stimulating as well. Where else can you, God-like, create different worlds and different people?

Review of What We've Done

In this chapter we've explored how we can use our own life experiences as a basis for writing fictional stories. We've looked at the elements of story and discussed how we might manipulate them as we create short fictional pieces. Reviewing the "visual mapping" strategy we've used in earlier chapters, we've seen how that brainstorming and idea-generating technique can be of use to us when thinking about fiction. Lastly, we've also focused again on various aspects of effective writing, for example, writing strong openings, using specific and descriptive language, and always considering possible alternatives when choosing words, phrases, and images. I encourage you to write fictional stories, but be careful. Once you begin, you might become addicted and find it impossible to stop!

We'll move on now to a form of writing that many Seniors find not only addicting but charmingly practical as well, and that is the writing of picture books for grandchildren and other little folks.

CHAPTER TEN

Children's Picture Books

Introduction

I hope Chapter Nine has inspired you to write fictional stories on a regular basis. As I stressed, stories are imaginatively stimulating and fun. Another specific type of story writing—whether fiction or non-fiction—is the children's picture story book. Many of the Seniors with whom I've worked like to try their hands at writing such stories. They find that these books make great gifts for their grandchildren, great-grand-children, and other little folks. Moreover, they are another way of passing on your stories, wit, humor, and creativity to future generations.

"But I can't draw!" is a comment I sometimes hear when I suggest writing picture books to a group of Seniors. And I always remark, "You don't have to know how to draw." Of course if you have artistic abilities you'll be able to create lovely watercolor, pastel, crayon, or ink illustrations to accompany your story. If you're like me, however, one with little drawing ability beyond stick figures, then you'll make use of other illustrations. That's what we'll highlight in this chapter: making use of photographs to write picture story books. I'll also offer at the end of the chapter some other suggestions for illustrating your books. Let's look first at some features of a picture story book.

Picture Story Books

Picture story books can be enjoyed by people of all ages; indeed, think how many of us still like to read or hear Dr. Seuss's *Green Eggs and Ham*: "That Sam-I-Am, That Sam-I-Am, I do not like that Sam-I-Am!" Picture story books, however, are particularly written for young children, say from birth to eight or nine years of age. Often these books not only introduce children to the world of imaginative literature, but also serve as a bridge to their independent reading. A good, "child-friendly" picture book has certain characteristics. Let's review them.

Picture and Text

In a picture story book both the illustrations and the text are important. For beginning readers, the pictures are more important than the text; they will carry the story for the young child who might be able to read only some of the words. Thus, when writing a picture story book, it is important that you make *a close tie between the illustration and the text* that accompanies it. The beginning reader should be able to figure out what the words say by looking at the illustration.

Predictable Language

The text on any given page should be short and should support the beginning reader in various ways. You should *not* write "Dick and Jane" or "See Spot run" kinds of sentences! However, your sentences should not be overly long and convoluted. For example, here is a sentence that would *not* be child-friendly: "The little boy whose Leggos were stacked into a firehouse took them apart to build a bridge." This would be better: "The little boy stacked his Leggos into a firehouse. Then he took them apart to build a bridge."

You should choose your words carefully as you consider the age of the child or children for whom you're writing the book. This does not mean "dumbing down" and using only very short words or commonplace vocabulary. We want to introduce children to vivid and colorful words and help them expand their growing vocabulary. Thus, I might want to expand a sentence such as "The girl picked a red rose" into "The girl picked a ruby-red rose." In doing so I'm not only expanding the child's background with different kinds of reds, but I'm also creating a pleasing sounding sentence, that is, the "r" sound in "ruby-red rose."

Repetition of words, phrases, and sentences throughout your story will also make it more child-friendly. The more times the child encounters a word, phrase, or sentence the more likely he or she will be able to read it. Thus, for example, a story about a little boy who has several adventures with his grandmother might include at the conclusion of each adventure a sentence such as: "And the little boy liked that!" Important, new, or unique words should be repeated in a natural way in your story. Don't, for example, introduce "rhubarb" in a garden story and then never mention it again.

Quite often *rhyme* in a story makes it easier for a child to read. This is especially true for very young children. End rhyme is probably the most predictable for children. The *couplets* that we wrote in Chapter Five on form poetry work very well here. For example, something like the following might support the illustrations of a little girl holding a rose to her nose and then putting the rose in a vase:

The little girl picked a ruby-red rose,
And she held it up to her pretty nose.
It smelled as sweet as her mother's perfume,
So she took the pretty rose up to her room.

Notice that I'm using rhymed couplets and that I'm also using repetition with "her," "she," "pretty," and "rose."

Plot

Picture stories for children should be relatively straightforward in terms of the plot. Your story should have a clearly identifiable beginning, middle, and end. The conflict that drives your story along should be evident and not overly complicated. Moreover, the characters, setting, and resolution to the conflict or story problem should be within the child's experiential, intellectual, and emotional grasp. I'll stress once again: Less is more!

Let's Write Picture Story Books

Before we explore the use of photographs as the basis for our picture story books, let's try our hands at writing the text for a very short three-page illustrated book. I'm going to use three figures from a computer clip art program. I've numbered them pages one, two, and three.

Page One

Page Two

Page Three

As we see in these three simple illustrations, we have a single *character* wondering what to do. That's the *conflict* or problem in the story: he doesn't know what to do. In the second page we see the character gets a bright idea. In the third page we see the *resolution* to his problem, and, that is, he has found another *character*, a friend, with whom to play. Thus, we have a very simple story with a basic *steady state*—

conflict—resolution—steady state chain. Now let's play around with some possible texts to accompany each illustration.

Page One

I'm going to write a possible line to accompany the illustration, and then I'd like you to write one. Try to make yours different from mine. I want you to see that we can write several different texts for any illustration. Okay, here's mine:

The little boy didn't know what to do.

Before you move on be sure to write your line. You did? Fine.

If you were writing this for a particular child, say your grandson or granddaughter, you might change this line to read:

Michael didn't know what to do.
or
Kathleen didn't know what to do.

Try changing the line you wrote by adding the name of a particular child.

We can expand or make richer the character in this little story by adding a simple adjective:

Lonely Michael didn't know what to do.

Try that with yours.

Let's add a second line to page one. I'm going to use a *rhymed couplet.*

Lonely Michael didn't know what to do.
He was home by himself and felt so blue.

Add a second line to your text for page one. It doesn't necessarily have to be a rhymed couplet. Remember that the text to the story should tie closely to the illustration. Okay? Once you've done that, let's move on to the second page.

Since we've started with two lines in page one, it will be more predictable and child-friendly if we stick with two lines for illustrations two and three. And since I used a rhymed couplet with the first illustration I'm going to do the same thing with the other two pages. I'm going to write my next two lines, and I'd like you to do the same with the text you're constructing for this little picture story.

Lonely Michael got a bright idea.
He'd call his friend, Roberto Rivera.

I'm using the actual names of children; thus, Michael would readily recognize the name of his friend, Roberto. Notice how I've used repetition with "Lonely Michael." How's your text for the second illustration? Do you have two lines? Did you use repetition, if possible? Does the story tie closely to the illustration? Now let's each do two lines for the last illustration.

They played all day along the lake shore,
And Michael wasn't lonely anymore.

I used repetition again, that is, "Michael" and "lonely," but I varied the way I used the two words. I also tried to use some sound patterns that would make the lines pleasant to the ear: "pl*ay*ed" and d*ay*"; and the "l" sound in "played," "all," "along," and "lake." I hope you can see that even in such a simple text to such a simple story for a beginning reader, we can still think about and use all of the good writing techniques we've explored in previous chapters.

I'd like you to review the lines that you've written for this three-illustration story. Read them out loud. Do they flow? How would they sound to a little child? Do your lines capture what's in the illustrations? Is there anything you might change to make the text more child-friendly? After you have played around with the first text you've written for these illustrations, I'd like you to take some time and write *different* lines for the story. I'd like you to see that you always have options when creating texts for illustrations. Take your time. Once you have completed the second text, come back to this chapter. You might want to take a break of a day or so before you do.

Using Existing Photographs

We have some options when we want to use photographs to write a picture story book. We can base our story on photographs that we already have, or we can take specific photographs for the particular story we have in mind. Let's look first at using existing photographs.

In Chapter Seven we explored various ways of writing about photographs. We can now use all of the ideas and strategies we played with in that chapter. The main difference is that this time we will pay special attention to our *audience*, and that is a young child or children. We'll typically use several pictures to tell a connected story. Moreover, we have the option of writing a non-fictional story about the pictures or a fictional one. Let's assemble some photographs and try our hands at two different stories, one non-fictional and one fictional.

I'd like you to look through your photographs and find at least four related pictures. You might use more, of course; it depends on how long you want your book to be. They might have been taken at the same time, or they might have been taken at different times but are related in some way. For example, you might have photographs of a particular 4th of July family gathering, or you might have photographs of such gatherings over many years. The pictures might include you as a child, the child or children for whom you are writing the book, contemporary photographs of you, and so forth. The possibilities are limited only by the photographs you have at hand. I'm going to use five photographs of my wife when she was a child as the basis for this story. Once you have selected your pictures, we'll continue.

Let's lay out our photographs and see how we might use them to write a *non-fictional* story. Turn the page to look at mine:

Now let's play around with possible arrangements which will tell a non-fictional story. I'm going to try this arrangement with my photographs:

1

2

3

4

5

Remembering the elements of story (steady-state—conflict—resolution—steady-state) and child-friendly language we explored above, let's each write a first draft of a text for the pictures. Take your time, and when you're finished, return to mine below.

1) Cheryl loved to play at Grandma Pearl's house. She went there in the winter.

2) Cheryl went to Grandma Pearl's house in the summer too. They worked in the flower garden together.

3) One year Grandma Pearl moved away to live with her four sisters. Cheryl missed her and was sad.

4) Grandma Pearl moved back home the next Christmas. She took Cheryl to meet Santa Claus.

5) Now Cheryl could play at Grandma Pearl's house again. She was happy.

How's your first draft? Let me briefly point out what I did with mine. First, I have a very basic plot with a simple conflict, that is, Cheryl's grandmother moves away, and a simple resolution, that is, the grandmother returns. Second, although I'm not using any sort of rhyme, I am trying to make the text predictable to the child reader by using two sentences for each picture. Notice too that I've made my text more child-friendly by writing simple sentences in the *active voice* ("She took Cheryl to meet Santa Claus") and not in the *passive voice* ("Cheryl was taken to meet Santa Claus"). Third, my sentences are closely tied to the photographs. Fourth, I've tried to use repetition (Grandma, Pearl, Cheryl, house, play) and contrast (sad/happy, winter/summer). All of these things will make the story more accessible to the beginning reader.

Look over your first draft. Are there things that you might change? Play around with your photographs and text until you have something you like. Then let's take the same set of photographs and write a *fictional* story about them. I'm going to rearrange mine for this story.

1

2

3

4

5

1) Once upon a time, there were five sisters, Pearl, Paula, Minnie, May, and Mary. They wanted children but had none.

2) A little orphan girl named Cheryl lived in a foster home. She wanted a mother of her own.

3) She asked Santa if he could bring her a mother of her own. He said he'd try.

4) On Christmas Day, Cheryl went to live with Pearl, Paula, Minne, May, and Mary. Pearl had adopted her.

5) Now Cheryl had a mother of her own. She was happy.

I've taken the same photographs, rearranged them, and composed a fictional story. Notice the story elements (plot, conflict, resolution, and so forth) and the other features (for example, repetition) that I've tried to use to make the story more child-friendly. I could probably arrange these photographs in a couple of other ways to make up different stories.

Look over your fictional story. See if there's anything you think you might change to make it stronger. Remember to read it *out loud* to hear how it sounds. Does it flow? Is there a rhythm to your writing? If you have a chance, read your story to a child. What's his or her response? (That's the best measure of your story!) Don't be afraid to ask the child what he or she thinks might make the story more interesting or easier to read. Quite often we get some of the best ideas from children.

Using Existing Photographs, Again

So far we've gotten a little practice with a three-page cartoon story, a non-fictional piece based around some of our own photographs, and a fictional story about those same photographs possibly rearranged. I hope you're developing a sense of how to think about pictures and accompanying stories for children. Once again, we want close connections between the pictures and texts; rich, vivid language that is child-friendly and repeated in various ways; simple, vibrant sentences that do not confuse the beginning reader; straight-forward plots (steady-state—conflict—resolution—steady state); and *complete* stories that can be read to or by the child in one sitting. It's better to write a too-short story than a too-long one. (You know my mantra by now: Less is more!)

Let's take a new set of photographs and apply much of what we've explored in this chapter and other chapters in the book. I'd like you to select at least five, or more, *recent*, or relatively recent, photographs (perhaps of yourself and others) that you think might lend themselves to a *fictional* picture story for children. Once you have those photographs, return here and we'll continue.

I've selected nine photographs of a trip my wife and I took to the Lofoten Islands in Norway; they are one of the world's great cod fishing areas. I think I can base a fictional story around them. Here they are in no particular order:

I've spread out the photographs in front of me, and now I'm going to use them to brainstorm some ideas using our Reporter's 5 W's & H format. Spread out your photographs, and on a fresh sheet of paper generate your ideas along with me.

My Photograph Ideas

The trip my wife and I took to the Lofoten Islands in Norway

Who

Cheryl
People aboard ship
Man at car rental agency
Cod fishermen
Cod

What

Cheryl on coastal ship trip

Sightseeing
Eating in a fine restaurant
Working on a cod fishing boat
Driving a rental car
Losing her purse
Stacking cod to dry

Where
Lofoten Islands in Norway
Fishing village
"Lofoten Guest House"
"Midnight Sun" coastal ship
"Tove" fishing boat

How's your brainstorming and listing coming so far? Notice how I've simply listed ideas by looking at my photographs. They (the photographs and ideas) are in no particular order yet. Let's continue with the rest of the Reporter's 5 Ws & H.

When
February or March
Prime cod fishing season in the Lofotens
Recent time (a new, 2000 model, automobile)

Why
Cheryl wants to visit the Lofoten Islands
Enjoys herself on the ship
Sight-sees in a rental car
Loses her purse
Stranded in the Lofoten Islands
Has a fine meal before she returns to the USA

How
Finds a job on a cod fishing boat
Helps to stack cod to dry
Makes money

As I'm brainstorming my ideas in the Reporter's 5Ws & H manner, a possible fictional story is already taking shape. You probably also have an idea for your story. Now, using our ideas, let's each specifically state our general story *plot* (steady state—conflict—resolution—steady state). Here's mine:

Steady state
Cheryl on a vacation to the Lofoten Islands

Conflict
Loses her purse and is stranded

Resolution
Gets a job with the fishermen and makes money

Steady state
Continues vacation and returns to the USA

This is a very basic plot, one which I think will work well. Before you read on, I want you to make sure that you have stated specifically your plot elements. Once you have them written down, let's both play around with various arrangements of our photographs. I've decided on the following for mine:

1

2

3

4

5

6

7

8

Now, with our photographs arranged in front of us, let's each write a first draft of a text for each of the pictures. Remembering the importance of a strong opening sentence or sentences, let's pay special attention to the way we begin our stories. I'm going to write three openings for my first picture. I'd like you to do the same for yours. Here are mine:

9

1) The coastal ship cruised along the Lofoten Islands in Norway. It's one of the world's most beautiful places.

2) It was spring, and the coastal ship "Midnight Sun" entered a small harbor in the Lofoten Islands.

3) In spring the sun still shines on the mountains at 10 p.m. in northern Norway!

These are three possibilities. I don't like the first one because there's nothing special about it; it's rather "flat." I like parts of both two and three, and I'm going to combine them into an opening for my first picture:

1) The coastal ship "Midnight Sun" entered a small harbor at 10 p.m one evening. The sun was still shining on the mountain peaks of the Lofoten Islands!

What I've tried to do in this first draft is to connect the ship "Midnight Sun" to the growing light above the arctic circle in spring and to identify both the ship and the place—Lofoten Islands. I think the photograph and text will capture the child's interest and encourage him or her to read on.

Look at your three possible openings. Read each out loud. Which one sounds better? Which is most vivid? Which one do you think will grab the child reader's attention? Might you combine the best elements of two or more? Maybe you'd like to write a totally new opening; if so, try it. Once you have a first draft for your first picture, let's move on and each write the accompanying texts for the next few photographs.

2) Cheryl was excited to be in a cabin on the "Midnight Sun." She always wanted to take a ship trip to the Lofoten Islands in Norway.

3) When the "Midnight Sun" docked in the harbor, Cheryl rented a small car. She wanted to see as much of the Lofoten Islands as she could.

4) But a terrible thing happened on her third day there. Cheryl lost her purse and all her money while looking at cod fishing boats in a small harbor.

How is your story shaping up? Notice what I'm doing with mine. I'm keeping the text to each photograph limited to a couple of sentences, and I'm using the active voice. I'm trying to link one page to the next by using repetition of specific names ("Midnight Sun," Lofoten Islands, Cheryl) and general terms (ship, harbor). Moreover, I'm aware of how I might make the text more child-friendly through rhyme ("ship trip") and sound ("on her third day there": the "th," "er," and "d" sounds working together). Look at some of these elements in your own story. Once again, be sure to read out loud what you've written. Then let's continue with the rest of our respective stories.

5) *Cheryl asked one of the cod fishing boat captains for a job. He said, "Sure, I can use all of the help I can get!"*

6) *Cheryl helped the captain catch thousands of cod. She also helped him hang the fish to dry.*

7) *It was hard work, but Cheryl liked hanging the cod to dry. The cod rack looked like a huge house.*

8) *The captain told Cheryl the cod would hang for three months. That's how they dry the fish in the Lofoten Islands.*

9) *Cheryl made a lot of money working for the fishing captain. He bought her a big dinner before she got back on the "Midnight Sun." She had a wonderful time in Norway, but she was excited to return home to the United States.*

Let's Take a Break

My first draft is rough, but in general I like the basic ideas in it. I've used repetition in a natural way, I think. I've included a bit of dialogue ("Sure, I can use all of the help I can get!") and I've used one simile to make the story more vivid ("The cod rack looked like a huge house."). Lastly, I bring the story back to the beginning on the "Midnight Sun" and Cheryl's desire to return home. (Most young children appreciate the fact that "there's no place like home.") I'm going to let this story incubate for some time, and then I'll return to it at a future date before I consider a final draft.

I'd like you to do the same with your photographs and story. Don't decide on a final draft just yet. Put it away for a while—at least a week or more. Then come back to it and look at it with all of the specific things in mind that we've discussed in this chapter and Chapters Seven and Nine. Of course, you might also gather some other photographs and begin new stories!

Sharing Your Picture Story Book

We won't go into a great deal of specifics about how to prepare your picture story for sharing with grandchildren and others. There are some simple things that you might do, however.

First, you can simply type or print your story on the necessary number of pages and tack the photographs above the text. Then you can make xerox copies and staple them together into a little book to share. This is the simplest book to make.

Second, and especially if your have color photographs, you can take your pages to a local copy shop and have the folks there reproduce them in color. A copy shop will offer a wide variety of paper color and quality. Moreover, it also will bind your book in one of several ways, for example, in a spiral binding. Using the services offered at a copy shop generally will result in a more "professional" looking book.

Third, computers, scanners, and digital camera technology offer many options. If you have expertise with one of the many desktop publishing programs available, you can lay out and print your own picture story book in a number of different ways. Using a scanner to copy and print your photographs or using a digital camera to make copies of your old photographs will enable you to manipulate text and photographs in a very sophisticated manner.

Fourth, if you are handy with particular arts and crafts, for example, drawing, painting, needle working, leather working, and so forth, you can illustrate and put together your own book in interesting ways. For example, you might add watercolor borders to each page, make a cover of cardboard and an attractive fabric, and then bind the whole thing together with needle and thread.

The key thing to keep in mind is the fact that your book is for a young reader or readers. Thus, you want to make it as visually attractive as possible; after all, it is a *picture* story book. If you want the book to last, then you must also consider ways of preserving it, for example, by laminating the pages and constructing strong front and back covers.

We'll continue later in the chapter with the publication and sharing of your picture story book. Let's consider first how we might think about and plan a picture story book when we haven't yet taken the photographs.

A Picture Story Book from Scratch

One of the valuable things about writing picture story books around photographs of ourselves is that it allows us to share our pasts with grandchildren and other young people. Building a story, either fictional or non-fictional, around, say, a set of photographs that show us as children or teenagers helps young people see us from a different perspective. It fosters the kind of intergenerational connections that are so important and yet so often lacking in today's world. As one young fellow commented after reading his grandfather's picture story book about himself as a child growing up on a farm, "Gosh, Grandpa, you really were a kid once!" Of course, the same thing applies to books we write about *our* own children when they were young; grandkids then are able to see their parents in a different light.

Another option that we have as Seniors is writing picture story books about the present, about our grandchildren and other young people as they are growing. This sort of writing is really for the future, a gift to those we might never know. Fifty years from now your grandchild might be sharing with *his* grandchild a picture story book that his grandmother wrote when he was young. Several Seniors with whom I have worked find this kind of writing the most rewarding. They regularly take photographs of their grandchildren, especially on such special occasions as birthday parties, vacations, "firsts," and so forth. They then use some of these photographs to document the occasion in story book form. These little books become favorites with the children as beginning readers.

Storyboarding

Writing picture story books from photographs that we have taken, say, of our grandchildren follows the same process we have explored above, that is, writing them as fiction or non-fiction, considering plot, choice of language, close connection between pictures and text, and so forth. The only difference is that when we are taking the photographs we have an opportunity to *plan ahead*. We can think beforehand about the photographs that would help make the best story book. (However, I'm *not* suggesting that you, say, artificially orchestrate a child's fourth birthday party into a staged photography session!) Such planning helps us be alert for possible moments that we might want to capture on film.

Storyboarding is a strategy that helps us do such planning. It is a technique used by television and movie directors and by those media professionals who develop slide shows and other visual presentations. It consists of using story cards to sketch out the visuals or photographs that we want to use. In essence, it allows us to tell our story visually before we have written the text. It is really a simple process. The story cards are three-by-five, four-by-six, or five-by-eight index cards which we use to sketch out the possible photographs that we want to take. Each card consists of a minimal drawing (perhaps nothing more than a stick figure) and a few words. A set of storyboard cards allows us to think about how we want to write our story and what variations we might consider. Together let's plan a set of storyboard cards.

I'd like you to get some index cards. I personally prefer four-by-six cards because they give me more space than three-by-five cards but are not as hard to manipulate as the larger five-by-eight ones. Use whatever works for you; however, it's important that you use some sort of card. You must be able to move around the cards as you consider possibilities. I'll sketch out my storyboard below, and I'd like you to sketch yours on your cards. I'm going to storyboard the photographs I might take at a child's fourth birthday party. I'd like you to select a particular event at which you might take some photographs and then use them as a basis for a non-fictional story book. Don't continue below until you have decided on such a specific event.

Okay, you have a particular event in mind? Great! Let's continue. I'm going to sketch my first story card for the photographs of the fourth birthday party. Don't do yours yet. First see what I've done.

1

Here's my first card. I'm thinking of taking a photograph in front of the house or apartment building at which the fourth birthday party is going to take place. Perhaps I might get a couple of shots showing adults and kids entering the building. This might serve as a beginning to my picture story book. (Think of it as the "steady state" we explored above.)

Now sketch out your first story card. Notice I simply have a brief drawing and a few words. All I want is something which might guide my photography. Once you have your first card, let's each do a second.

2

My second story card shows a picture of my grandchild, Mary. She is the central figure, or character, in this story, and thus I want to highlight her at the beginning.

Do you have your second card? Fine. Let's each complete the next two or three.

3

4

5

My third, fourth, and fifth story cards remind me that I want to capture the people who are at the party: the other children, parents, and, certainly, myself! How are your cards coming? Are you trying to *visually* see how your picture story book might go? Let's continue.

6

My sixth card is the "resolution" to the disrupted steady state of the story. The "conflict" or "problem" of the story, so to speak, is that everyday life has been changed by Mary's fourth birthday celebration. It is resolved or acknowledged by the singing of "Happy Birthday" around the cake.

7

8

9

That's my storyboard for the birthday party. I will build my picture story book around these photographs. They remind me of the pictures I will want to take while at the party. Once again, however, I will take them in a "natural" manner. I will not go around arranging everyone into artificial groupings! I

10

11

will certainly take more photographs, and I might not use all eleven in the story. Nevertheless, I will have a general sense of my non-fictional story and the photographs to support it when I begin to write.

Notice too the value of story *cards*. They give me the option of moving them around to see how I might structure my story differently. For example, I can arrange cards three, four, five, and nine in any number of different ways. Story card ten, the photograph I'll have someone take of Mary and her friend, might also work in any number of different places. Indeed, it might serve as the cover or front page of the story of Mary's fourth birthday party.

Look over your story cards. Do you see different ways by which you might arrange them? Might there be something important that you have forgotten in this event? Might you want to add one or more story cards? As you are visually planning the photographs you will take and the picture story book you will write, do you see the key elements of story, that is, some steady state, plot consisting of a conflict and resolution, and a new steady state?

Now the best way to experience the value of storyboarding and writing a picture story book from photographs you take is to go out and do it! The event around which you develop the cards, photographs, and stories does not have to be a "major" one such as a birthday party. It might simply involve a visit to a park or a trip to the local ice cream parlor. It might consist of only four or five photographs. What I'd like you to do is to sketch out some cards, take the photographs, and then use them as a basis for a picture story book. I'm sure you'll be happy with your results!

A Little More on Sharing Your Picture Story Books

In this chapter we've been focusing on the use of photographs in the writing of picture story books for children. There are many other possibilities, however. Depending upon your particular talents, you might use your own drawings or paintings instead of photographs. You could use a range of media, for example, crayons, colored markers, charcoal, oils, watercolors, and so on. Or you might think about using a variety of paper, pictures, and lettering to make a collage book. One woman in one of my writing groups wrote a fine picture book based around cut-out shapes she made from different colored construction paper. Regardless of the medium you use, photographs or, say, geometric shapes from construction paper, the process we've explored above will remain the same.

Lastly, simply because you do not have grandchildren does not mean you can't write picture story books. Most pre-school, day-care, and elementary school teachers and children's librarians at the public library welcome Seniors into their classrooms and storytelling sessions. They are eager to help children make the kind of intergenerational connections I mentioned earlier. Sharing your own picture story books with small groups of children in an informal classroom setting or at your local library is a most rewarding thing to do! Give it a try!

Summary of What We've Done

In this chapter we've built upon the ideas we explored in Chapter Seven, Writing about Photographs and Chapter Nine, Fiction; we've also utilized many of the strategies we developed throughout the book. We have seen how pictures and texts might go together to create lively books for young children. The particular features of books for young readers were highlighted. We have also seen that sharing and publishing possibilities are numerous.

Let's now move on to the next chapter to a very different kind of writing, and that is the keeping of diaries and dream journals.

CHAPTER ELEVEN

Diaries & Dream Journals

Introduction

I have stressed throughout the various chapters the importance of considering your purpose and audience as you write. Why you're writing something and who will read it will determine how you go about creating a particular text, whether it is an memoir, poem, or work of fiction. In this chapter we will focus on writing for a very specific audience, and that is ourselves.

Most Seniors with whom I have written over the years have kept some sort of diary or journal at some time in their lives. Indeed, one woman I know has kept a brief daily journal for over forty years! Sometimes we start a diary and write in it faithfully for a period of time but then abandon it; and then sometimes we return to it. Sometimes we keep a journal during intense times of our lives, for example, during an illness or after uprooting ourselves and moving to a new part of the country.

There is no particular way to approach diary and journal writing, and you might prefer not to keep one or to keep one sporadically. I myself keep a journal whenever I travel and am away from home, but I seldom write in it while I am at home. There is no "right" way, and there is no need to feel guilty if you at this point decide to stop reading this chapter. However, I think you will find it interesting and potentially enlightening to continue and to try your hand, however briefly, at keeping a diary or journal.

Why Keep a Diary or Journal?

People often make distinctions between diaries and journals, but for our purposes we are going to use the two terms synonymously. Diaries are typically thought of as places to record one's personal, deepest, or "secret" feelings. Journals, on the other hand, often have a number of different purposes, for example, to record observations while walking in the forest, to capture ideas and insights for future use, to clarify one's thinking, to simply keep in the habit of writing something on a regular basis, and so forth. I'm going to use the word "diary" from this point on to refer to any record that we keep, for any purpose or purposes, regularly or sporadically, in which we might write extensively or simply jot down notes to ourselves. The key point is that the audience for the writing is ourselves.

Because diaries are private, we can be (often brutally) honest in them. We might use them to vent our anger at, say, an overbearing or insensitive neighbor. We might express our sadness or disappointment over a child's failure in marriage. On the other hand, we might use the diary to capture the sheer magic we feel after stepping out on our front porch after the first snowfall. All of these private emotions might find their way into a diary. However, overheard conversations, witty expressions, sudden insights, and particular moments that we want to remember might also find their places in a diary. Subsequently we might "mine" our diaries for the "ore" of ideas, words, phrases, and images which we will then use in our poems, memoirs, and stories.

Let's Try Keeping a Diary

The format of our personal diaries will vary from individual to individual and even within the individual depending upon the time and place. As I mentioned above, there is no "right" way to keep a diary. For example, I keep a spiral notebook while I'm traveling, but if I'm out of town for longer periods of time I will keep a running diary on my computer. Some Seniors I know will only write longhand in an "official" diary (with lock and key!) while others will use only the computer. A friend of mine carries a little notebook in his shirt pocket in order to be able to write immediately when he has an idea or hears something he wants to remember. He has scores of these notebooks filed in his home. I suggest you try a couple of ways to keep your diary. You'll find what works best for you.

Keeping a Simple Diary

I'd like you to keep a diary for at least three days; use any format you choose, that is, notebook, computer, and so on.

Write in it at the beginning of the day, at the end, or at any time you feel that you have something you want to preserve for later. You *don't* have to worry about spelling, punctuation, complete sentences, or "proper" English! Remember, a diary is for *yourself*; thus, it can be as correct or as sloppy as you want it to be. Lastly, each entry does not have to be long. Some days we have a lot to write, and on other days we might have little. Just give it a go for a few days! Come back here after that.

How did your diary-keeping go? Was it difficult? Did you find yourself writing at any particular time of the day? What kinds of things did you record? As an example, here are three entries from the diary I kept while on a brief trip to London during the early winter months of 2000. I was alone and had just arrived from Oslo, Norway.

2/26/00
6:35 p.m. Room 3—Ebury House Hotel—London
Arrived yesterday afternoon—hotel has changed—or I have—seedy, run-down, but fairly clean—tiny room on Ebury—noise—no chair—writing this on the bed
Walked last evening—sad & blue—dinner at Indian restaurant Cheryl and I ate at near Victoria Station—mediocre and high-priced
Went to Globe—tour—exhibition—well-done—then to Westminster—long lines to get in—5 pounds!—didn't go
Walked St. James park—our "old route"—to Green Park to hotel—Flowers Blooming!! Daffodils, crocuses, buds on some trees—grass is green—joggers in shorts & t-shirts—around 50f, but a sense of Spring!

Bright gaudy yellow walls of this old room—contrast with live yellow of the daffodils

Now off to the theater and Beckett—in a really great mood!!

Notice my particular journal style. I seldom use complete sentences; instead, I jot down words and phrases. (I've cleaned up my spelling here. In my spiral notebook I have several misspelled words.) Notice too that there are no great insights here. I'm simply recording where I am, some of the things I did, how I'm feeling, and some images that struck me (spring and yellows in the park contrasted with the gaudy yellow wallpaper in my room). Here's my entry for the following day.

2/27/00

9:45 A.M. in Room 3—Ebury House

Just finished breakfast—dreary basement room—a family of hung-over Brits talking about last night's party— manager of B&B complaining about too much work—old owners sold out 3 years ago, thus the run-down condition

Beckett's "play last night—powerful, tedious performance—the dreariness, hopelessness of one's life, but ultimate bravery: "I'll go on"—Go on to what?

Afterwards dinner at "Chinese Dragon"—pretty good food

Street musicians, performers (guy with some bike trick; a fire-eater—did Cheryl and I see him years ago in York?)— ***Chinese men and women stopping people and giving them back massages—guys curled on the streets asking for money

Crush on the tube trying to get home

Now—9:57—off to Westminster for 11 a.m. service— then to Blake's grave and British Museum

I wrote this second London entry in my diary in the morning after breakfast. I was jotting down what occurred the evening before. Notice again that it is a mixture of the commonplace (just finished breakfast), observations (guys curled on the streets), insights I got from the play by Samuel Beckett ("I'll go on"), and an image that struck me as unique and which I might use later, in a poem perhaps (Chinese men and women stopping people and giving them back massages). I typically put asterisks *** in front of something that I might want to easily pick out later. Now here's my third London entry.

> *2/27/00—Room 3—10:03 p.m. Ebury House*
> *Just got back from "The Shakespeare"—the best fish and chips! Great with a couple of pints!*
> *Today first to St. Mary's for a sung mass—then to Bunhill Fields and Blake's grave*
> *British Museum—apocalypse exhibit closed—browsed—Elgin Marbles—lunch where Cheryl and I ate in cafeteria*
> *Walked Green Park back to Ebury—Images:*
> *Young couples—20s/30s—***one young couple walking under gnarled tree propped with large iron brace—she with a cane—bent over—moving very slowly—step by step—he holding on to her arm—helping:*
> *What do they think? Feel? She? He?*
> *My old poem of guy and wife in St. James*
> *Bunhill Fields: Large Monument:*
> *Here Lyes Dame Mary Page*
> *March 4, 1728*
> *In the 56th year of her age*
> *In 67 months she was tapd 66 times*

And taken away 240 gallons of water
Without ever repining at her case
Or ever fearing the operation
All around cemetery—buildings—more building— tower cranes—walls
Large patches of crocuses: yellow, purple, pale blue— under ancient oaks—snowdrops violet and cream
***Daffodils/crocuses/thorny bushes nearby Blake's grave with new leaves
At his grave:
4 potted plants—votive candles—a fabric red rose tied to multi-colored scarf (yellow, red, blue) held on top of Blake's tombstone by large stone—also a red carnation next to fabric rose
***On way back stopped at St. James Church where Blake was baptized—inner-city church—committed church— listened to two guys play—piano & violin—a repetitive, sweet, few chords—evocative—amateurs—peaceful, soothing, moving—Sudden Blessing!

As you can see, this was my second diary entry for the day; thus, I wrote one in the morning and one in the evening on February 27, 2000. This entry contained more than the previous two. Since I have a love of the great English poet William Blake's work, obviously I was inspired to write more. Notice also how I actually copied the words on a tombstone which caught my eye. Finally, one young couple out of many struck me with their obvious difficulty and love; they reminded me of another such couple my wife and I once saw in a London park.

I'm sharing entries from my personal diary—my audience now has moved beyond myself—in order to provide a few simple examples of how I (one particular person) keep it. I hope you see that my diary contains a variety of things, and most of them are not especially profound or literary. It contains documentation and memory aids of where I've been and what I've done, observations, quotations, and some images that I might at some point put into other writing. A diary is a cache, a place for ideas; it can be whatever you want it to be. If you find yourself interested in keeping a diary, then I strongly suggest that you continue building on what you've already started.

Keeping and Using Targeted Diary Entries

We can also use a diary for more specific purposes, for example, to gather observations, words, and images which we will then use as a basis for other kinds of writing. One of the activities I ask Seniors in my writing groups to do is to keep a record for a certain period of time of interesting, unique, or moving things they observe. I tell them that these do not have to be anything out of the ordinary; they simply have to be something that strikes a chord in the soul, for example, a cardinal burning red in the sunset or a sudden smile on a grandchild's face. We can then use the diary to focus our attention, to help us look more closely at the world around us. Once we have gathered several pages of such observations, we then "mine" them for poetry, stories, or memoirs.

And that's what I'd like you to do for the next week or so: Use your diary to notice more closely the world around you. As you go through your daily rounds, pay special attention to what you see, hear, and feel. Try to make at least a few brief entries in your diary every day. Once again, they do not have to be long, but try to make them specific and vivid enough so that you can use them to re-create a particular scene or event. That, for example, was what I was trying to do in one of my diary entries above:

> *Young couples—20s/30s—***one young couple walking under gnarled tree propped with large iron brace— she with a cane—bent over—moving very slowly—step by step—he holding on to her arm—helping:*
> *What do they think? Feel? She? He?*
> *My old poem of guy and wife in St. James*

Take a Break

After at least a week, or longer if you so choose, return *here* with your targeted diary entries.

How did it go? Did you gather a number of words, phrases, images, sounds, and other things in your targeted diary entries? You should have at least a few pages of entries with which to play. If you don't, then continue to gather them before we go on.

I'll share some targeted diary entries of my own as examples. The first comes from several days at a street fair in Tucson, Arizona a year or so ago. My diary entries run on for over ten pages. Here is a brief section:

> *. . . and then the food stands: at every intersection of 4th Avenue and another street all of the food stands: draft beer stands, hot buttered corn-on-the-cob stands, Mexican: fish tacos, regular tacos, fajitas of one kind and another, Greek:*

salads, gyros, lamb plates; Indian: fry bread: with powdered sugar, as a taco smeared with beans and cheese and sauce; fried foods: french fries, onion rings, burgers, hot dogs, chili dogs, brats grilling, popcorn, ice cream, yogurt, wine from local wineries ($2.00 a glass or buy it by the bottle), fresh lemonade (one guy complaining that it's nothing but water and lemon juice). . . and among the food different attractions: women from 30 to 70 dressed in red, white, and blue outfits with stars on their vests, living American flags, dancing. . . .

As you can see, what I was doing was trying to capture what I was experiencing as I strolled though the street fair. I stopped several times with a soft drink or a beer and wrote quickly in my notebook.

Here is a second targeted diary entry that I wrote while I was teaching for a brief time in Ghana, West Africa. My wife had just arrived from the USA, and I took her from Cape Coast where we were living out to the fishing village of Elmina. I carried my notebook with me and wanted to capture the sights, sounds, smells, and life of the village.

Elmina—Cheryl's first chance to get to a village market— smells of fish, rotting vegetables, human waste—fish market: load/unload fish—buy and sell—shining in the sun—one kid with two long pike-like, barracuda-like fish—holds them up to me—walk through town—castle in the distance— warm breeze—outdoor restaurant: fish-flake soup, rice, Club beer cold—pineapple lady—bought one—fan palms—sudden shower—glorious, refreshing in the heat—tro-tro taxi back to Cape Coast. . . .

Let's "mine" one of our targeted diary entries for some "gold," or at least "silver." I'm going to make a list of some words and images from my Elmina entry. I'd like you to look through your targeted diary entries and select one that you think might be fruitful. Then, as we have done many times before, let's make parallel lists.

My Targeted Diary Entry
Smells of fish/rotting vegetables/human waste
Fish market
Kid load/unloading fish
Two pike-like/barracuda-like fish
Castle in the distance
Warm breeze off ocean
Restaurant—palm plaited
Rickety chairs
Fish-flake soup
Joloff rice
Club beer—coaster to keep flies off
Old woman selling pineapple
Slices of fresh fruit
Rain suddenly—sweeping inland
We dance in the puddles
Fan palms swaying
Black & white crows cawing
Tro-tro (old VW bus) packed back to town
Hot, crowded: cool skin on skin—black on white

That's my list. As you know by now, once we start listing, more ideas and images come to mind. I used my targeted diary entries as a catalyst for my memory. The more I jotted down images, the more I remembered and the more specific

I became (for example, "joloff rice" instead of just "rice," and the tro-tro as an "old VW bus" and not just a "tro-tro taxi"). I'm sure the same thing occurred with you as you began to make your list.

At this point we can turn to any one of the previous chapters and use our lists to write a poem (form poem or otherwise), fictional piece, picture book for our grandchildren, memoir, and so forth. We won't work on these pieces together, but I'd like you to get at least a first draft of *some* piece that you will share with a wider audience than yourself. My objective here is to help you see that you can use a personal diary as a basis for more public writing. I'm going to play around with my list and try to develop a poem. When you have a first draft of whatever you choose to write, return here. Don't rush, and come back when you're ready (even if it's days later).

Time for a Break?

You're back? Great. Here's what I did with my list from our trip to Elmina:

At the Fish Market in Elmina, Ghana
I Remember My Grandfather, Forty Years Dead
Palm-plaited baskets piled
With small, silver-sided fish,
Sparkling in the sun like the old
Silver dollars my grandfather
Gave me as a gift one Christmas,
Which I polished and cherished
Until I lost them at sixteen
In an all-night poker game;
Already losing their luster

As the flies begin to settle,
And the women handle and hawk
Them to the haggling passersby.

A toothless boy of nine or ten
Digs in one basket and offers
A long slender turquoise fish:
Its open mouth frozen in death,
Baring the teeth of northern pike
We used to catch in Wisconsin,
And whose heads my grandfather
Mounted on his apartment wall.

I hold its stiffened body
And study it in my hand:
It is sticky and smells of sea,
Death and old silver dollars.
I buy it from the curious boy
Who laughs excitedly as I
Throw it into the lagoon
And watch it float steadily
Seaward in the outgoing tide.

The two fish that the kid held up to me proved to be the basis of my poem. That single image took me from Ghana to my youth, my grandfather, the past, and then back to Ghana again. Those simple jottings I made in my targeted diary entry led eventually to this poem which I personally like.

I've shared my diary-based writing with you, and now I'd like you to be sure to share what you have written with at least one other (preferably more) person. Then we'll try a second kind of targeted diary, one I call an "eavesdropping diary."

Keeping and Using Targeted Eavesdropping Diary Entries

Carl Sandburg, the poet who wrote about Chicago with its "big shoulders" and hundreds of other poems, once commented that people talk poetry every day without knowing it. All you have to do to catch that poetry, he said, is to listen closely. That's what an "eavesdropping diary" is: A tool which helps you listen closely and capture the unique language of people around you. Most Seniors with whom I've written have enjoyed trying such diaries, and some have continued to keep them long after we have begun to focus on other kinds of writing.

A small pocket or purse notebook is perfect for this kind of diary. It allows you to jot down surreptitiously conversations, expressions, phrases, and words that you might overhear in, say, a restaurant, grocery store, or other public place. What you want to do with such a diary is to note anything that you hear others speaking which you find interesting, unusual, funny, and so on. As we discussed above, what we're doing with such a diary is developing a cache of language which we can later mine for our writing.

Some examples from the writing of Seniors in my classes include: "Women—they always want something!" "Swearing doesn't do a damn bit of good and sounds like hell!" "It isn't every day I get to stand by a pretty flicka [girl]." "His thinking is as tangled as a pile of spaghetti." "I was out in the boonies on business." "Bailing out the biffie"; "a whippletree and a willowy woman"; "zocks and callabuttons"; "noodie noddie" (a person without focus or conviction); "Seven devils!" The Seniors in my classes captured some of these in their diaries because they thought they were interesting, funny, or simply because they liked the way they sounded. (I especially like "a whippletree and a willowy woman.")

I'd like you to keep an eavesdropping diary for a period of time, say a week or two. Whenever you're out, listen to the ambient talk around you, whether in a store, on a bus, in a park, or at a social gathering. The more you listen, the more you will hear; Sandburg's emphasis on spoken poetry will become evident to you. Try to jot down immediately or shortly after hearing it any word, phrase, or sentence that you find unusual, witty, or interesting. Be as secretive or as open as you'd like. (I've even had one Senior in a class ask a stranger to repeat a phrase that she wanted to write down in her diary!) Once you have at least ten to twenty entries in your diary return here, and we'll then work briefly with them. Good listening!

Using Eavesdropping Entries

I hope you had fun eavesdropping and now have a stock of "spoken poetry" from which to draw. As we did above with our targeted diary entries, let's select one or perhaps a couple of related entries that we'd like to develop into a more extensive piece of writing. Let's begin together brainstorming and listing ideas and images.

My Eavesdropped Entry or Entries
"Dog it off!"
"Don't know their ass from their elbow!"

I was walking past a construction site and stopped to watch the men at work. I heard one burly man in a hardhat yell "Dog it off!" to the crane operator who was unloading a steel girder from a truck. "Dog it off" means to stop immediately. The young man atop the truck who had hooked the

278 Exploring Our Lives

cable to the girder had done it incorrectly, and the girder was in danger of slipping free and possibly injuring someone. The burly man then said in disgust to another worker, "These kids don't know their ass from their elbow!"

I jotted these two expressions immediately in my notebook. I had not heard "Dog it off" in over forty years, not since I had worked as a laborer in construction during my summer vacations. The burly foreman's comments brought to mind a number of memories. I'm going to continue brainstorming; you do the same.

My Eavesdropped Entry or Entries

"Dog it off!"
"Don't know their ass from their elbow!"
Summer laborer jobs
A skinny teenager
Inexperienced
Not as strong as the other men
Scrapping steel beams
Grinding weld spots
Made many mistakes:
Stacking steel incorrectly
Pouring concrete on the street
Cutting lumber unevenly
Supported by older men
Often chided by foreman
All appreciated my tenacity
Red lead paint mist in the air
Rust in my eyes
Exhausted at the end of day

These are some things that I remember from my own experiences working as a teenager in construction. Try to generate at least ten specific ideas or images under your eavesdropped entry or entries. Then let's both use our entries and items from our lists to write a short poem. (If you'd like later to write a different or longer piece, that's fine. However, let's give a short poem a go here.)

I'm going to begin my poem with one of the comments made by the foreman. Why don't you try to start your poem in the same fashion?

"Dog it off! Dog it off! Dog it off"

I'm repeating the man's exclamation for dramatic effect and because I want to begin my poem with a line of between eight and ten syllables. How's your first line? Say it out loud. Do you need to turn it into two lines or more? Might you modify it in order to make it sound or flow better? You don't have to write *exactly* what you heard! Let's continue developing our poems now by using ideas from our brainstormed lists.

"Dog it off! Dog it off! Dog it off"
The foreman cried to the crane
Operator pouring yards of concrete
Out of the forms and into the street.

I'm using the expression I jotted in my notebook along with a *specific* experience I remember having, and that is failing to position the huge concrete bucket full of fresh cement over the wooden forms into which it was supposed to go. Instead, I had the concrete running over the street. Notice in my poem I'm trying to stay with roughly the same line length in terms of syllables and I'm also using an end rhyme (concrete/street) that seems to naturally work. Look over your developing poem. How does it sound? Might you *naturally* use some rhyme? Any words to change? Are you capturing a *specific* scene or event? Let's continue with our respective poems.

> *"Dog it off! Dog it off! Dog it off"*
> *The foreman cried to the crane*
> *Operator pouring yards of concrete*
> *Out of the forms and into the street.*
> *I stood by watching helplessly*
> *As he and a laborer named Ray*
> *Skillfully swung the bucket past me*
> *And brought it to rest on the ground.*

I'm continuing to develop this little event (though it wasn't "little" for me at the time!). Since this is an unrhymed poem, I'm also paying attention to other ways to make it sound poetic, for example, the "r" sound in "laborer named Ray" and the "s" sounds in "Skillfully swung." I don't remember the laborer's name, but I'm using "Ray" for its sound effect. Might you modify anything in your poem to make it sound better?

I'm going to end my poem now by using the second targeted expression.

> *"Dog it off! Dog it off! Dog it off"*
> *The foreman cried to the crane*
> *Operator pouring yards of concrete*
> *Out of the forms and into the street.*
> *I stood by watching helplessly*

As he and a laborer named Ray
Skillfully swung the bucket past me
And brought it to rest on the ground.
"These damn college kids got to go!"
"They don't know their ass from their elbow!"

Notice how I've included a line that I did not hear or jot in my notebook: "These damn college kids got to go!" I'm adding that for a couple of obvious reasons. First, it identifies me as a student (and I'm using "college kids" instead of "high school kids" for the sound). Second, I want to end the poem with a rhyme: go/elbow. I think I'll title this poem, "Summer Job." However, as usual, I'm going to let it incubate for some time before I come back to it and perhaps rework it.

Once you have a first draft of a poem that you like, put it away. Come back to it later and see it again. You might also want to look through your eavesdropped entries and try playing around with one or more in poetry, or fiction. Even if you don't keep a specifically identified eavesdropping diary, keep your ears open in the future for the spoken language of people around you, the poetry that people talk daily. Now let's move on to a very different kind of diary, and that is the dream journal.

Dream Journals

As we age we quite often sleep less or less soundly and wake up in the middle of the night. A writer in one of my groups began one of her poems with these lines: "Last night as I lay on my bed/Many thoughts went through my head." Doug Nielsen began his funny poem "Cremation" with these lines: "At 3 A.M. all I was thinking/About was cremation."

Another writer described how she used to wake up in the middle of the night and then lay worrying about her health and financial situation. Things changed when she began to keep a diary by her bedside in which she would jot down ideas for poems and stories or would try to capture the images that were still fresh from a dream. These wide-awake-in-the-middle-of-the-night times now became for her fruitful occasions for writing.

In this section I'd like us to explore a specific kind of personal diary, and that is the dream journal. We'll see what such a journal is, what value it might have for us, how we might use it to better understand ourselves, and also how we might use it to capture our dreams in a more extensive and expressive piece of writing.

Why Keep a Dream Journal?

Dreams come to us from our "underworlds," our inner selves with which most of us rarely come in contact. Dreams tell us of our night worlds, our hidden thoughts, and deepest longings. We know that Freud wrote extensively about dreams and their possible meanings. Unless you happen to be a psychologist or one especially interested in the interpretation of dreams, I don't necessarily recommend a great deal of reading and study of them. That's not my purpose for suggesting a dream journal. Rather, I see such a journal as an opportunity to help us get glimpses into our "night selves," become more skilled at recognizing rich images, and utilizing dream images in our writing.

Imaginative psychologists who follow in the work of Jung say that we should focus on the *images* in our dreams. They say that by exploring and playing with the images of a dream in various ways we are able to gain deeper insights into it than if we try to figure out what the "story" of the dream "means." Thus, our dreams become opportunities for us to poetically capture our hidden and barely recognizable night selves. Keeping a dream journal is similar to the act of writing poetry.

How to Keep a Dream Journal

We all have experienced numerous times in our lives when we have had a pleasant or frightening dream that was so real we awoke in the middle of the night joyous and laughing or trembling with fear. We immediately told ourselves that we wanted to remember the dream so that we could share it with someone in the morning. However, in the morning the only thing we were able to remember was whether the dream was pleasant or unpleasant. The rest of it was gone.

If we want to capture our dreams, then we must do so *immediately* upon having them, that is, as soon as we wake. The way to do this is to keep a notebook or pad of paper and pencil at our bedside along with a table lamp or a small flashlight. When we wake from our dream we can immediately jot down a few words, phrases, or images from the dream. When we wake up in the morning, we are then able to use those words, phrases, and images to reconstruct the dream. This takes a little practice, but the more we do it the easier it becomes. Moreover, strange as it may seem, when we focus on capturing our dreams we find that we are able to actually wake ourselves after a particularly rich dream. Our night selves more readily communicate with our day selves.

Here's an example of brief notes I made immediately after waking at 2:30 A.M. from a particular dream:

> *backside of earth—gobi desert—bleak—train overhead on bridge—3 priests—whiskey priests—no shirt—god's will—I play*

When I awoke in the morning, after breakfast I sat down with these briefest of notes and reconstructed the dream in the following manner:

> *I'm on the backside of the earth. It is barren and bleak. I see the Gobi Desert with all of its desolation.*
>
> *Then I see overhead a train, an old steam locomotive, on a very high bridge which arches over an immense gulf. The bridge is a bright pink.*
>
> *I walk the railroad tracks and come upon three Catholic priests playing miniature golf. They are grizzled, unkempt, red-faced, and the sort of whiskey-priests we had in the old neighborhood or that one would find in a novel by Graham Greene.*
>
> *One of them doesn't wear a shirt but instead has a black sash wrapped around him. He is loose-fleshed, pale, and like the other two an unhandsome man.*
>
> *I watch them play the game, and with every stroke they make they say, "Oh, this is God's will! Thank God!" I say to them, "It's not God's will; it's luck." We argue, and I challenge them to another game. I beat them in nine holes.*

I'm sure you see that from my sketchy 2:30 A.M. notes I was able to capture the dream. But more. As I thought and wrote about it after breakfast I *re-created* it and made it richer and more vivid than it might have been as I dreamt it. I don't remember if in the dream the one priest was "loose-fleshed," but as I wrote about him that image surfaced. I didn't think about Graham Greene's novels in the dream, but I did make the literary connection as I wrote about it. And I don't remember responding to the priests in the dream; I merely challenged them to a game of miniature golf and won. Saying "It's not God's will; it's luck" is something that naturally came as I wrote, and I think it gives the dream more resonance.

Thus, that's the process of keeping a dream journal: Training yourself to wake immediately after an especially vivid dream; jotting down in a bedside notebook enough words, phrases, or sentences to help you remember the dream in the morning; and then working with your notes after you wake up in order to not only reconstruct the dream, but also to re-create it in a poetic manner.

Keeping a Dream Journal

I'd like you to begin keeping a dream journal for a certain period of time, say at least a couple of weeks. It will take a while for you to get into the habit of waking and immediately jotting down words and images from your dreams. Then I'd like you to work with those notes later in the day; the morning is the best time while everything is still fresh. However, that's not always possible. Try though to re-create in your journal each one of the dreams from your brief notes. After you become comfortable with the process and have ten or more dream entries, return here, and we'll work together on one dream.

Working with a Dream

How did you find the experience of capturing your dreams? Did you find yourself becoming more alert to them as time went by? Was it difficult to turn on the light and write in the middle of the night? For many people it is easier to roll over and go back to sleep; however, that usually results in the loss of the dream. Did you find yourself developing and "fleshing out" the dream as you wrote about it? That I think is the most important, interesting, and creative part of the whole process. Remember, we're not concerned with explanations of the images and the events in our dreams. I, at least, am not a psychologist. Rather, we're concerned with using those images as a source for our writing and as a means of communicating with another part of our selves, our night selves.

Together let's work with a single dream. Select one of your dreams that you found especially interesting and on a separate piece of paper work alongside me.

Dream Notes

> old bike—troop street—archer—mares drugstore—friends—majariks—jack martin and old merc—catch a ride—class—crazed navy guy—horrid—can opener—hide blanket over head

These are the notes I wrote after waking from an especially vivid dream. I find the dream interesting because it involves my youth, my immediate past, and my present as a university teacher.

Do you have your dream notes? How do you jot them down? Any particular way? I usually write mine without any capitalization and use dashes between each word or words. Of course, I'm fixing the spelling here; in my dream journal *many* words are misspelled, but as we know that's not important. You might find a particular way to write your notes, or you might find yourself capturing them differently on different nights. *How* you write them is not important; *that* you capture them is.

Let's use our dream notes to write a dream vignette, one that tells an image-rich story. We'll focus on all that we've explored in previous chapters, for example, a strong opening, rich language, vivid closing, and so forth. Let's each start with an opening paragraph. Use your notes but also use your creative imagination to develop the paragraph.

> *I'm riding down Troop Street from 29th to the old neighborhood on a black-and-gray Schwinn bicycle with a rusty, clanking chain. I turn down Archer Avenue and pedal up to Mares Drugstore where I meet some of my high school friends. They're still teenagers, but I'm an adult close to sixty. I don't know what we're up to, but we walk down the street past Majarik's Furniture Store and over to St. Bridget's schoolyard.*

How's your opening paragraph? Notice what I've done with mine. I've "fleshed it out" with specifics that I think will make it more vivid and lively: the "old bike" of my notes becomes "a black-and-gray Schwinn bicycle with a rusty, clanking chain"; and my "friends" are now "still teenagers, but I'm an adult close to sixty." I'm using my dream and dream notes as a basis for this particular vignette.

Look over your opening paragraph. Have you built upon your notes? Is there anything you might change to make your opening more descriptive? Are you using *specifics*? Say your paragraph out loud. How does it sound? Are your sentences lively and for the great part in an *active voice*? Play around with the paragraph, and then when you're ready let's continue to further develop our respective vignettes.

I'm riding down Troop Street from 29th to the old neighborhood on a black-and-gray Schwinn bicycle with a rusty, clanking chain. I turn down Archer Avenue and pedal up to Mares Drugstore where I meet some of my high school friends. They're still teenagers, but I'm an adult close to sixty. I don't know what we're up to, but we walk down the street past Majarik's Furniture Store and over to St. Bridget's schoolyard.

Jack Martin, an ex-colleague of mine who has been retired for over ten years now, is in the schoolyard with a candy-apple red 1957 Mercury. It's a monstrous hulk from days long gone, and a pair of red-and-white sponge dice dangle from the rearview mirror. A suicide knob with a picture of a bikini-clad blonde is coupled to the steering wheel.

Jack says that we have to get to class, and he offers to take us there. He opens the trunk, and it is loaded with tools, snow tires, and a wooden crate of empty quart soda bottles. There is still room for my bike, and I comment about the size of the trunk. "They don't make them like this any more," I say.

We arrive at the university, and I get to my class as the bell rings. I'm teaching a literature class of some sort, and all of the students are young except for a retired Navy veteran. He's a poor student who doesn't attend class regularly. I don't like him and his aggressive manner.

I've continued with my vignette by expanding those brief notes from my dream journal. I'm also making the logical temporal connections that weren't there in my dream or notes. Moreover, I'm adding some dialogue to make the piece more lively.

Look over your vignette-in-process and see if at this point in time there are things you might add or change. These are first drafts, however, and we don't want to be overly concerned with what we have now. We can always work with the piece later. Let's continue and complete the drafts of these vignettes.

I'm riding down Troop Street from 29th to the old neighborhood on a black-and-gray Schwinn bicycle with a rusty, clanking chain. I turn down Archer Avenue and pedal up to Mares Drugstore where I meet some of my high school friends. They're still teenagers, but I'm an adult close to sixty. I don't know what we're up to, but we walk down the street past Majarik's Furniture Store and over to St. Bridget's schoolyard.

Jack Martin, an ex-colleague of mine who has been retired for over ten years now, is in the schoolyard with a candy-apple red 1957 Mercury. It's a monstrous hulk from days long gone, and a pair of red-and-white sponge dice dangle from the rearview mirror. A suicide knob with a picture of a bikini-clad blonde is coupled to the steering wheel.

Jack says that we have to get to class, and he offers to take us there. He opens the trunk, and it is loaded with tools, snow tires, and a wooden crate of empty quart soda bottles. There is still room for my bike, and I comment about the size of the trunk. "They don't make them like this any more," I say.

We arrive at the university, and I get to my class as the bell rings. I'm teaching a literature class of some sort, and all of the students are young except for a retired Navy veteran. He's a poor student who doesn't attend class regularly. I don't like him and his aggressive manner.

The Navy vet begins to shout obscenities and threatens the students sitting around him. I try to intervene, but he gets up and goes on a rampage, attacking people with a "church key" can opener. I watch in horror as he strikes it across the face of a young woman and shouts, "The sun ain't yellow!"

The crazed man then turns toward me, and I try to hide. There is a pile of blankets in the corner of the classroom, and I take one of the blankets and put it over my head. I think that if I can't see him he won't see me. I stand stock-still and wait. I hear him breathing next to me, but he does nothing. We both stand and wait.

That's a first draft of my dream vignette. Again, I focused on specifics, added dialogue, and ended the piece in a state of expectation. For a first draft I like the way it sounds as I read it out loud. What does it mean? I don't know, and I don't really care. As I highlighted above, I'm not a psychologist, and that's not my purpose for capturing dreams and writing about them. I simply like the way my night self has brought this dream and vignette to my day self. I would never have written this piece if I had not been open to the images of my dream.

Once you have a first draft of your dream vignette, you can, as usual, put it away for a while, work on another draft immediately, or, if you choose, simply abandon the piece as one more exercise that you do not want to pursue. Regardless of your choice, I hope you see that keeping and using a dream journal is a viable practice that you might want to continue in the future.

Summary of What We've Done

In this chapter we've explored the purposes and possible importance of keeping various kinds of personal diaries. We've tried our hands at daily diaries, targeted diaries, eavesdropping diaries, and dream journals. All of these diaries initially have a particular audience, and that is ourselves. We have seen however that we can also use these personal texts to create more public pieces of writing. While diaries aren't for everyone, they do provide us with a space for communicating with ourselves and for gathering images and ideas. Keeping a diary even for a short period of time, say, while on a vacation, can be a most useful and engaging practice. I encourage you to keep one even sporadically in the future.

We are now coming to the conclusion of this book. Let's move on to the last chapter and some final comments and suggestions.

CHAPTER TWELVE

Writing Groups and Writing Resources

Starting a Writing Group

Chances are that you're reading this book at home. Hopefully you've been taking my advice and reading your various pieces of writing out loud, whether they are prose vignettes, poetry, short stories, or sketches about photographs. *Hearing* our writing almost always helps us improve it. Likewise, I hope that you've been considering the purposes and audiences for your writing and have been sharing your efforts with family, friends, and the larger community. Although personal and sometimes intensely private, writing is ultimately social in nature: We write to be read by others.

For many people, the process of writing itself is also social. Talking about topics, sharing works in progress, eliciting suggestions on how to make a particular piece stronger, and getting praise and encouragement from others in a supportive group setting tend to make our writing stronger and, if nothing else, almost always make it more fun to write. The poet Kenneth Koch once observed after conducting poetry workshops for ill and disabled folks in a nursing home that such collaborative efforts fostered a "slightly festive atmosphere" in which the participants were able to laugh and share in the excitement of creation.

During the last two decades in my own work with Seniors I have found Koch's observation to be true. Participants in writing groups tend to write more, more consistently, and on a greater range of topics than those who write alone. The solidarity that develops over time among members of a writing group fosters a healthy openness and serves as a catalyst for new ideas and insights. It often does more, however. As a participant in one of my current writing groups observed, "We know more about one another and we talk about more important things than we usually do with even our own family members." Another fellow commented, "You know, all of you are my therapy group!"

Obviously, I wrote this book for Seniors who want to explore different kinds of writing on their own. I stressed in the Introduction that "most likely [you] have your own particular purpose for reading this book." For some readers the reasons for using this book include the desire to write independently. Some people by inclination or experience simply want to work alone or work better alone, and that's fine. My own experience has shown me that some individuals do *not* profit from participation in writing groups. Each person must discover that for him- or herself.

I also wrote in the Introduction:

"Looking at a particular event in our lives, say, our first love, through a written memoir, short story, or poem, gives us various angles from which to see the event. . . . I hope as you read this book you will try forms of writing that might be new or even strange to you."

I firmly believe that sharing with others in supportive group settings will make it more likely that you will try new and even strange forms of writing. As a woman in one of my groups laughed many years ago, "I didn't want to write haiku, but that's what everybody was supposed to write for our next meeting. I didn't want to be the odd one out, so I wrote some. Now I can't stop writing the damn things!"

In the following I offer some brief suggestions for those who are interested in forming a local writing group. Of course, people are different and each situation will be different; therefore, my suggestions are only general guidelines. I believe that they will be useful in most settings.

Finding Fellow Writers

A colleague and I once talked sadly about "closet poets." We had just started a poetry writing group at the Senior center in a small village in southern Illinois. I don't think the population was more than five hundred. The individuals who joined the group had lived in the area for most of their lives, and for a couple people that meant seventy years and more. When we started to share our writing most of the people in the group brought in notebooks, folders, and even shoeboxes of writing that they had been doing for years. What was lamentable was the fact that they were surprised to see what the others had brought. These friends and neighbors who had lived together in the same town for many years did not know that they all wrote poetry!

I can guarantee that there are other Seniors in your community who like to write with others or who would like to write if they had the opportunity and support. All it requires is for someone to take charge and ask! I have formed all of my writing groups over the years simply by asking. Try one or more of the following:

a) Talk to the director at your local senior center, community center, retirement village, assisted living facility, service organization, or other place where Seniors gather and ask her or him to post a notice and talk with individuals who might be interested in forming a writing group. Have the director set a time and date for an organizational meeting. Tell her or him to stress that the meeting is an informational one and that no one has to make any commitment. You and/or you and a friend then will have to conduct the meeting to see the level of interest, set possible meeting times, and select a convenient venue.

b) Post a notice in your local weekly newspaper, church, synagogue, or mosque newsletter, or, if you have one in your community, on a local radio program that makes public service announcements. In my town, for example, there is a weekly "Senior Focus" program on an AM station.

c) Contact your local Historical Society; most counties or regions have one. Generally, people who participate in activities at such societies are interested in exploring the past, both their own and others, for example, oral history tapes often are housed at such places. Ask the director or coordinator to post a notice and to allow you to talk at one of the regular gatherings.

d) Lastly, contact the folks at your local bookstore and check to see if there are any book discussion groups that meet there on a regular basis. If so, ask if you might talk to the members for five or ten minutes concerning the possibility of a writing group. Often people who participate in book clubs are the same ones who are eager to join writing clubs.

Depending upon which of the above approaches you use, you will most likely attract different people. Do you want a writing group that consists only of Seniors? Then you will probably advertise at the local Senior center. Do you want a mixed-age group? Then you might place a general notice in the local newspaper. Moreover, your particular notice can specify an age range, say, fifty-five years of age and older. There are advantages to both single age, that is, fifty-five or sixty and older, and mixed aged groups. You and the members of the group will have to decide which works best for all of you. In one of my present groups a woman sometimes brings her granddaughter and grandson to the weekly meeting. Having a pre-teen and teenager participate in the group adds a particular, and enjoyable, flavor to the gathering.

How to Begin

Let's say that you and five or six other interested people have gathered for your first meeting. How should you begin? After sharing introductions and possible goals, the first thing the group needs to do is to set a regular meeting time and place. I recommend meeting every week or, at least, every other week for an hour or an hour-and-a-half. Writing groups that gather once a month tend to have a more difficult time developing a sense of community and maintaining a vital sense of interest among all participants.

"Grounds rules" should be established early in the group's formation. In my writing groups we have a basic tenet: "Never apologize" for a piece of writing. Whenever someone attempts to apologize before s/he shares something ("Now, I know this isn't very good. . . ."), one or more members of the group will say, "Remember, no apologies!" The no apology rule highlights the fact that if we are writing on a regular basis we usually will write a wide range of texts: some will be "good," some mediocre, and some might even be "bad." As I stressed in Chapter Two, the important thing about writers is that *they write*.

Another item that might be explored is the amount of time each person has for sharing his or her writing. I have found that discussing this early on prevents problems later. Some individuals naturally talk more than others, and some people write much longer pieces than others. By setting a general time limit for each individual, say, five to ten minutes, the group will enable all participants to have an equal and un-rushed amount of time for sharing and for receiving responses to his or her writing. After all members have shared, there usually will be more time for additional readings.

The *kind* of responses individuals want to their writings also should be discussed. Unwanted advice should be avoided. There is no surer way of alienating individuals or of ultimately causing the disillusion of a group than to allow negative comments and harsh critiques. I strongly recommend "appreciations" after each person's reading, that is, a highlighting of something that other members enjoyed in the piece of writing. If an individual desires some specific advice, s/he should ask the other people in the group to pay particular attention to those aspects about which s/he wants feedback, for example; "Listen to see if I have created a clear picture of my father"; or "Let me know if I have used too many adjectives in this poem"; or "I'm not sure if the last part of this vignette really connects with the earlier parts; let me know what you think."

The structure of each meeting also might be discussed. How does the group want to spend the hour or hour-and-a-half? Some groups will spend the first thirty or forty minutes sharing what members have written since the last meeting. They then will devote the rest of the time to discussions of craft, for example, issues of grammar and punctuation, word choice, or how to make a piece stronger by paring it back. Other groups simply will devote the total meeting time to sharing and discussing the participants' writings. There is no "best" format. Each group will decide for itself what members want to get from it.

Finally, the group might want to discuss how topics are generated for mutual writing. Often viable ideas surface during the course of a meeting. A story someone shares, for example, about a close brush with death, might resonate with all of the other participants, and that will be the writing assignment for the next meeting. Sometimes current events suggest possible topics. These can be as dramatic as the terrorist attacks on 9/11/01 or as personally memorable as the music and death of jazz singer Peggy Lee early in 2002. Group members might take turns suggesting topics. And of course the many ideas for writing that I offer in this book can provide topics for a long time.

Publishing the Group's Work

A group that meets regularly for a year or so will soon produce many pieces of prose and poetry. I have found that it is exciting for all members to have a selection of the group's writing gathered and published. Moreover, such publications help to further strengthen group solidarity and often attract new members. Some guidelines that I have found to be effective include:

1) Have one group member collect a copy of all the writing that is shared at each meeting; these pieces can be kept in a folder, filing drawer or box;

2) After a year or so, decide on two editors who will go through the collected works and select a representative sample from all writers, for example, three or four pieces from each participant; these should include both prose and poetry;

3) Elicit volunteers from the group or hire someone (for example, high school students) to type clean copies of the selected works;

4) Seek out someone with desktop publishing skills or go to your local copy shop, say, Kinko's, and have the booklets assembled with appropriate illustrations, photographs, clip art, and so forth;

5) Advertise the booklet in your local newspaper, at the community center, and other appropriate venues;

6) Contact your local bookstore and hold an "Authors' Party/Reading" of the booklet.

Writing Resources

I and others have found that models of prose and poetry often provide viable resources for writers; this is especially true when participating in a writing group. I often bring into my groups pieces of writing by diverse authors. We read and discuss them and then look at those aspects of a particular writer's work that make him or her unique. We then attempt to shape a piece of writing in the author's style. Playing around in different styles and with different kinds of texts helps us develop our own particular strengths and styles.

Each group will have its own favorite authors that members might want to imitate. A few models that I have found to be effective over the years include the following:

Prose: *The Complete Short Stories of Ernest Hemingway.* Regardless of what one might think of Hemingway as a person, his short stories, especially the early Nick Adams stories, are models of how to write clear, clean, and lean prose. Trying to write in Hemingway's style helps one learn that "less is more."

Poetry: *The Essential Haiku: Versions of Basho, Buson, and Issa,* edited by Robert Hass.

The Voice That Is Great Within Us: American Poetry of the Twentieth Century, edited by Hayden Carruth.

These two inexpensive paperback collections offer writers a wealth of examples of poetic styles to explore. Both collections are edited by major American poets. Hass' collection is a fine complement to the haiku section in Chapter Five, and the poets in Carruth's collection offer examples that can be used in connection with the poetry writing in Chapter Nine.

How might you use these models in a writing group? I have found the following format to be helpful:

1) Read the prose piece or poem out loud; read it a couple or several times;

2) Observe what is unique about the particular piece, for example, its form, imagery, sentence length, punctuation, and so forth;

3) Make notes next to the piece as you think about it;

4) Share and discuss individual observations in the group;

5) Using the prose piece or poem and the various observations about it, write your own piece that is similar in some way, again, in form, imagery, and so forth;

6) Share the individual works in the group.

Memoirs & Life Vignettes: The great oral historian Studs Terkel offers innumerable examples of how to capture in writing both spoken language and one's own life stories. His books are not only models, but they also serve as catalysts for exploring particular topics and historical periods. Five of his works that I have found useful are:

The "Good" War: An Oral History of World War II;

Hard Times: An Oral History of the Great Depression;

Working: People Talk about What They Do All Day and How They Feel about What They Do;

Coming of Age: The Story of Our Century by Those Who've Lived It;

Will the Circle Be Unbroken? Reflections on Death, Rebirth, and Hunger for Faith.

Writing Handbooks & Reference Works: I have not stressed the "mechanics" of writing in this book. My primary purpose has been to engage you in many different kinds of writing. That is not to say that such things as correct spelling, punctuation, and "proper" grammar are not important. They are. However, they are only important when you have a draft that you want to publish for others to read. When you're working with a first or second draft, paying too much attention to such mechanics can actually get in the way of your writing. It's best to worry about such things *after* you have a draft of your vignette, poem, or story on paper. Get it on paper first and play around with the mechanics second. Moreover, it's important to remember that there is no one "correct" way to punctuate, capitalize, use grammar, or say anything. It all depends on what you're trying to accomplish with the piece of writing. There are certain "standard" guidelines and forms you might follow, and these are often very useful. Nevertheless, it doesn't mean that these "standards" are always right for your particular piece of writing.

There are many grammar and style handbooks on the market if you would like to explore such topics as punctuation and so forth in depth. You can find these at any large bookstore or through one of the Internet book companies; however, I strongly suggest that you find one that is short, simple, and helpful to you and your particular needs. You want to write—not study— grammar! Similarly, there are various spelling handbooks, and if you use a computer and word processing program then you will undoubtedly have a spell checker. I personally find that a good dictionary, say, one of the *Webster's Collegiate* dictionaries, usually has all I need in terms of spelling, punctuation, and so forth. The "Handbook of Style" in the back of the *Webster's* is a model of how to be brief and informative.

A "classic" handbook for looking more closely at one's writing and for exploring aspects of craft in the writing group is the book by William Strunk, Jr. and E.B. White: *The Elements of Style, 4ᵗʰ Edition*. This little book has proven over the years to be invaluable to many writers, both novices and those with much experience. I highly recommend it.

Two handbooks on effective use of grammar and punctuation that I especially like because of their specific straightforward explanations and examples and their macabre wit are by Karen Elizabeth Gordon:

The Deluxe Transitive Vampire: The Ultimate Handbook of Grammar for the Innocent, the Eager, and the Doomed;

The New Well-Tempered Sentence: A Punctuation Handbook for the Innocent, the Eager, and the Doomed.

Finally, I think all writers can benefit from owning and (carefully!) using a copy of *Roget's International Thesaurus*.

Final Advice

Like all advice from strangers who are not familiar with particular contexts and participants, the suggestions I offer above should be taken with care. These are things that have worked for me and others in specific situations and with specific individuals. Hopefully, they will work for you too. However, don't be afraid to modify them or to ignore what doesn't work.

Good luck!

Living with Grace, Force, and Fascination

We are approaching the end of our writing journey together, but hopefully it is not an ending; rather, it is a continuing and perhaps for some readers a new beginning. We have explored many different kinds of writing together and for many different purposes. Ultimately, all of the writing that we've done, whether memoirs, vignettes which will serve as a family legacy, poetry about important people, places, and things in our lives, personal diaries and dream journals, or picture books for our grandchildren, is, to quote William Carlos Williams again, "a sort of renewal." As a Senior moving forward into the last part of your life's journey, writing can help you make that journey purposeful, bountiful, exciting, and a gift to others. Writing in old age can help us live with enthusiasm. The great American poet Walt Whitman captures in his poem the importance of rounding one's youth, one's life, to a beautiful end with force and grace.

Youth, Day, Old Age and Night

Youth, large, lusty, loving—youth full of grace, force, fascination,
Do you know that Old Age may come after you with equal grace, force, fascination?

Day full-blown and splendid—day of the immense sun, action, ambition, laughter,
The Night follows close with millions of suns, and sleep and restoring darkness.

My purpose throughout this book has been to help you look closely at your life and the world around you with fresh eyes before the sleep and restoring darkness that inevitably comes to us all. Very few of us have lived lives that will be recorded in history books; however, we have all—in different ways—lived lives full of fascinating encounters and experiences. Your unique past, present, and years yet to come offer you an inexhaustible treasure trove from which to draw and create. Writing helps you exclaim, "Yes, what a life I've had after all!"

Making It Better

Throughout the various chapters we have explored those "basics" of good writing, including such things as strong beginnings and endings, cutting excess (less is more), using rich and vigorous vocabulary, utilizing the active voice over the passive, and listening to the *sound* of your writing. I have stressed the importance of going beyond a first draft if a particular piece is especially interesting to you and if you want a wider audience to read it. On the other hand, a first draft might be fine if you are your only audience or if you are quite satisfied with a first effort. (It happens!)

We almost always write for other readers. Without exception, the Seniors with whom I've written over the last twenty years all wanted their work to be shared and appreciated by others. More than a few came to my workshops because they had been writing poetry in secret and wanted an opportunity to share it with others. I was always pleased when, say, an eighty-year-old woman would bring in a box or folder of poems that she had written over many years. It likewise was sad to think that for all those years her friends and neighbors in her small town were unaware of the many lovely poems she had written. Our writing must be shared.

Regardless of whether we write with others or alone, it is vitally important to get feedback from others on our efforts. Finding a friend with whom you can share your writing in order to receive *honest* feedback is key to producing your best work. Sometimes we have different readers for different kinds of writing (for example, someone who likes memoirs and someone else who loves and reads a lot of poetry) and for reading our work at different stages of development. For instance, I always ask my wife to be the reader of a first draft because I want enthusiastic support regardless of the piece's overall quality. She gives me that. As I further develop the piece in subsequent drafts I will then ask her for more specific criticism and I likewise will ask other people to read it.

Your friend and reader does not have to be a literary critic in order to help you with your writing. All he or she needs to be is honest and willing to give you the kind of feedback you desire. And that's important: *You* need to ask your friendly reader for *specific* kinds of feedback. Of course, you'll start by asking your reader, "Well, how do you like it?" But then you have to be more particular. Questions such as these are generally helpful: "Is there anything confusing in it?" "Could you actually *see* any of the people, places, or things that I describe?" "Does the beginning grab you?" "Does the ending logically follow from what came before?" "Are there any words that you think I might change to make the piece stronger?" "Am I being too wordy?" "I've used rhyme in this poem. Does it sound natural or is it forced?" "How does the vignette sound when you read it out loud? Does it flow for you?" The more particular you are with the feedback you request, the more helpful will be the feedback you receive. Find one or two friendly readers with whom you feel comfortable!

Farewell

I'll conclude with a poem by Douglas Nielsen, an eighty-five-year-old member of my current writing group who died recently. He wrote this lovely poem to Dorothea, his wife for more than half a century. It captures for me the essence of what writing by Seniors can be: Expressions of joy, awe, and love. I wish you many hours, days, and years of good writing!

Feelings

Sitting in the porch swing holding hands has a feeling all its own. It's just you and me. Day's end is near. We watch the sun go down, and it's something to see: a gold ball reflecting on the clouds; gold and silver streaking the sky. A feeling of awe surrounds us, and a feeling of peace and joy is around us too.

We turn to the east and see the shadows and darkness creeping in. Then it's dark, and we can hardly see the shapes and figures passing. Lights start to show. Day sounds go away. Evening and quiet sets in.

The moon shines bright, and the stars shine too. We're still on the porch swing holding hands. I love you.

Books Available from
Santa Monica Press

Blues for Bird
by Martin Gray
288 pages $16.95

The Book of Good Habits
Simple and Creative Ways
to Enrich Your Life
by Dirk Mathison
224 pages $9.95

The Butt Hello
and other ways my cats drive me crazy
by Ted Meyer
96 pages $9.95

Café Nation
Coffee Folklore, Magick, and Divination
by Sandra Mizumoto Posey
224 pages $9.95

Collecting Sins
A Novel
by Steven Sobel
288 pages $13

Discovering the History
of Your House
and Your Neighborhood
by Betsy J. Green
288 pages $14.95

Exploring Our Lives
A Writing Handbook for Senior Adults
by Francis E. Kazemek
312 pages $14.95

Footsteps in the Fog
Alfred Hitchcock's San Francisco
by Jeff Kraft and Aaron Leventhal
280 pages $24.95

FREE Stuff & Good Deals
for Folks over 50
by Linda Bowman
240 pages $12.95

FREE Stuff & Good Deals
for Your Kids
by Linda Bowman
240 pages $12.95

FREE Stuff & Good Deals
for Your Pet
by Linda Bowman
240 pages $12.95

FREE Stuff & Good Deals
on the Internet
by Linda Bowman
240 pages $12.95

Helpful Household Hints
The Ultimate Guide to Housekeeping
by June King
224 pages $12.95

How to Find Your Family Roots and
Write Your Family History
by William Latham and
Cindy Higgins
288 pages $14.95

How to Speak Shakespeare
by Cal Pritner and
Louis Colaianni
144 pages $16.95

How to Win Lotteries, Sweepstakes,
and Contests in the 21st Century
by Steve "America's Sweepstakes
King" Ledoux
224 pages $14.95

The Keystone Kid
Tales of Early Hollywood
by Coy Watson, Jr.
312 pages $24.95

Letter Writing Made Easy!
Featuring Sample Letters for Hundreds of Common Occasions
by Margaret McCarthy
224 pages $12.95

Letter Writing Made Easy! Volume 2
Featuring More Sample Letters for Hundreds of Common Occasions
by Margaret McCarthy
224 pages $12.95

Nancy Shavick's Tarot Universe
by Nancy Shavick
336 pages $15.95

Offbeat Food
Adventures in an Omnivorous World
by Alan Ridenour
240 pages $19.95

Offbeat Golf
A Swingin' Guide to a Worldwide Obsession
by Bob Loeffelbein
192 pages $17.95

Offbeat Marijuana
The Life and Times of the World's Grooviest Plant
by Saul Rubin
240 pages $19.95

Offbeat Museums
The Collections and Curators of America's Most Unusual Museums
by Saul Rubin
240 pages $19.95

Past Imperfect
How Tracing Your Family Medical History Can Save Your Life
by Carol Daus
240 pages $12.95

Quack!
Tales of Medical Fraud from the Museum of Questionable Medical Devices
by Bob McCoy
240 pages $19.95

The Seven Sacred Rites of Menarche
The Spiritual Journey of the Adolescent Girl
by Kristi Meisenbach Boylan
160 pages $11.95

The Seven Sacred Rites of Menopause
The Spiritual Journey to the Wise-Woman Years
by Kristi Meisenbach Boylan
144 pages $11.95

Silent Echoes
Discovering Early Hollywood Through the Films of Buster Keaton
by John Bengtson
240 pages $24.95

What's Buggin' You?
Michael Bohdan's Guide to Home Pest Control
by Michael Bohdan
256 pages $12.95

ORDER FORM 1-800-784-9553

	Quantity	Amount
Blues for Bird ($16.95)	_____	_____
The Book of Good Habits ($9.95)	_____	_____
The Butt Hello ($9.95)	_____	_____
Café Nation ($9.95)	_____	_____
Collecting Sins ($13)	_____	_____
Discovering the History of Your House . . . ($14.95)	_____	_____
Exploring Our Lives ($14.95)	_____	_____
Footsteps in the Fog ($24.95)	_____	_____
FREE Stuff & Good Deals for Folks over 50 ($12.95)	_____	_____
FREE Stuff & Good Deals for Your Kids ($12.95)	_____	_____
FREE Stuff & Good Deals for Your Pet ($12.95)	_____	_____
FREE Stuff & Good Deals on the Internet ($12.95)	_____	_____
Helpful Household Hints ($12.95)	_____	_____
How to Find Your Family Roots . . . ($14.95)	_____	_____
How to Speak Shakespeare ($16.95)	_____	_____
How to Win Lotteries, Sweepstakes, and Contests. . . ($14.95)	_____	_____
The Keystone Kid ($24.95)	_____	_____
Letter Writing Made Easy! ($12.95)	_____	_____
Letter Writing Made Easy! Volume 2 ($12.95)	_____	_____
Nancy Shavick's Tarot Universe ($15.95)	_____	_____
Offbeat Food ($19.95)	_____	_____
Offbeat Golf ($17.95)	_____	_____
Offbeat Marijuana ($19.95)	_____	_____
Offbeat Museums ($19.95)	_____	_____
Past Imperfect ($12.95)	_____	_____
Quack! ($19.95)	_____	_____
The Seven Sacred Rites of Menarche ($11.95)	_____	_____
The Seven Sacred Rites of Menopause ($11.95)	_____	_____
Silent Echoes ($24.95)	_____	_____
What's Buggin' You? ($12.95)	_____	_____

Shipping & Handling:	
1 book	**$3.00**
Each additional book is	**$ .50**

Subtotal	_____
CA residents add 8.25% sales tax	_____
Shipping and Handling (see left)	_____
TOTAL	_____

Name —————————————————————————————————

Address ————————————————————————————————

City ——————————————— State ————————— Zip —————————

❏ Visa ❏ MasterCard Card No.: ————————————————————————

Exp. Date ——————————— Signature ————————————————————

❏ Enclosed is my check or money order payable to:

Santa Monica Press LLC
P.O. Box 1076
Santa Monica, CA 90406

www.santamonicapress.com 1-800-784-9553